Admirable Simplicity

GEORGE
WAYNE
SMITH

Admirable Simplicity

Principles for Worship Planning
in the Anglican Tradition

The Church Hymnal Corporation
New York

Table of Contents

Preface

THIS IS A HANDBOOK WRITTEN FOR THOSE WHO plan worship in parishes of the Episcopal Church, although others besides planners and Episcopalians may find it of value. The planning of liturgy is a daunting task, as conscientious clergy come to realize. So do many lay members of parish worship committees, once they begin to recognize the intricacies of the liturgical heritage and the complexities of parish life. It is never enough to do the "right" thing liturgically, for the "right" thing must also be received by a community. Careful planners learn both aspects of their work; the Prayer Book (and its tradition) and community. They discover that they must remain accountable to both.

I have written this handbook to help worship planners understand their work. It is an introduction only, and it is intended most of all to suggest some necessary questions for planners to ask and to point toward possibilities. If readers look to this handbook for a final word on the liturgy, they will be disappointed. The book describes principles, trends, and points of reference, and as you will discover, I do not mince words in my descriptions. But such plain-speaking should not suggest to the reader that this is a book of "answers" describing the "right" way to do Anglican liturgy. I hope that it becomes clear that there is no single "right" way for Anglican liturgy to happen and that, in fact, the Anglican way of worship is really a collection of idioms within a single language. It is the language itself, however, and not the separate idioms that provides the subject of this handbook. Thus partisan anglo-catholics and ardent evangelicals alike may be disappointed in this book, for neither idiom of worship, anglo-catholic or evangelical, is the subject of this work.

This work is unabashedly concerned with the Anglican ways of worship, and non-Anglicans may find this characteristic off-putting. I hope that the work is identifiably Anglican without lapsing into chauvinism or that worst of Anglican flaws, religious imperialism. I make no claims here about the superiority of the Anglican heritage of worship, only that it is my way of living as a Christian and the way of the larger communion of believers in which I live. There is no such thing as "generic" Christianity, and my hope for any non-Anglican readers is that they can glean an occasional insight from the Anglican language of worship to translate into their own idiom of offering praise to God.

I have written this handbook especially for the intelligent layfolk who faithfully serve on worship committees throughout this church of ours. I hope that this book is something they can read in an evening or two or three as an introduction to their work. I hope that the individual chapters will provide resources for their work as they address specific issues in shaping a parish's life of worship.

The title of this work comes from William Chillingworth, the English reformer who used the phrase "admirable simplicity" to describe his understanding of the Anglican way of worship. What I hope can become clear in this work is that simplicity does not have to be drab or boring or "low church." The admirable simplicity of the Anglican heritage is generous, rich, festive, and anything but dull.

The list of acknowledgments is not lengthy but necessary: the people of the Baptist churches in Ovalo, Texas, who first taught me the Jesus story, and in Tuscola, Texas, in whose community I received the gift of baptism; James Leo Garrett, Jr., who introduced me to the joys of serious study; George Udell, who welcomed me to the Anglican way of being Christian; the late William Weeks Eastburn, who modeled for me the life of pastor and liturgist; Louis Weil, who taught me to love the liturgy; the people of Good Shepherd, Brownfield, Texas, who helped me to understand that good liturgy has more to do with quality of life than with grandeur; the people of St. Christopher's, Lubbock, Texas, who showed at least one new curate the graces of good humor and much patience; the people of Emmanuel Church, Hastings, Michigan, who allowed me to minister with them and share their heritage of unpretentious and uncomplicated anglo-catholic fervor; the people of St. Andrew's, Des Moines, Iowa, who support my studies and who have shaped me in their own liturgical heritage of noble simplicity; Warner White, who has shown me the way to live well as a presbyter of this church; the bishops who have recognized my vocational yearnings as pastor and scholar and have encouraged me in that path, Sam Hulsey and Christopher Epting; my readers for this project at the School of Theology at the University of the South, Marion Hatchett and Donald Armentrout, great teachers who have helped me love more deeply this peculiar heritage of Anglicanism; the countless fellow presbyters in whose presence I have argued and hammered out the ideas in this book, especially John Stanley and Craig Gates, whose company on summer evenings at Sewanee became the occasion for new insights, and my colleagues close by, Charles Pope, Margaret Wilcox, and Kristy Smith, who are always generous with their friendship; a couple of deacons who remind me by their very being that the presbyterate is neither the sum nor the norm of Christian ministry, Susanne Watson and Peggy Harris; the libraries at the University of the South and Nashotah House, who have been openhanded in lending me priceless old books; the staff at Church Hymnal Corporation, especially Frank Hemlin and Frank Tedeschi; and the other people in my household: Debra Morris Smith, who is a loving and forbearing spouse (and always editor of first resort), Austin Taylor Smith, Geoffrey Lee Smith, and Laura Kathleen Smith, who delight me and help me keep life in perspective.

CHAPTER 1

The Anglican Way

THE REMARKABLE VARIETY OF LITURGICAL PRAC-
tices in the Episcopal Church leads many observers to assume
that most decisions about worship have to do with taste or personal preference. Subjectivity often rules, and even when planners
keep subjectivity in check, suspicions of subjectivity abound.
Parishioners frequently surmise that the proclivities (and even
idiosyncrasies) of their priest, more than anything else, set the
agenda for the parish worship. Clergy of every sort—evangelicals,
anglo-catholics, charismatics, liberals, and even rubrical fanatics
—often presume to have a right, based in the worship canons, to
superimpose their preferences on a parish, with little or no regard
for the traditions of that worshiping community or the greater
Anglican heritage. Does anyone expect to find a definable core for
Anglican liturgical practice beyond these subjective bases?

Moreover, the aesthetic issues often determine many of the
decisions about parish liturgy. A passion for "the beauty of holiness" has marked the Anglican way, but even this norm becomes
problematic in an age when a common language for describing the
good, the beautiful, and the true has collapsed. The worldwide

community of Christianity called Anglicanism lacks a consensus when it comes to aesthetic concerns, and this lack of consensus plagues our conversations when we gather to plan our liturgies.

In many parishes the liturgy becomes a focus for pastoral conflicts of every sort, a microcosm of other struggles around issues of authority, taste, propriety, and necessity. Many are the battles fought over music (renewal or traditional? hymnal or song-book? guitars or tracker organ? choir or congregation?), ceremonial (restrained or fulsome? modest or elaborate?), and language (Rite I or Rite II? Prayer Book or supplemental texts for inclusive language? or missal? or earlier Prayer Book?). The parish and the wise pastor learn together to navigate these unsettled waters and even to direct the energy from the storm into a kind of creativity. The unwary pastor, ill-prepared or thinking it possible to navigate the waters alone, will sink. Anglican liturgy depends heavily on the priest and pastor having a sense, even a charism, for planning the liturgy and presiding in it. But Anglican liturgy is more about the people than about the presider. From the first Prayer Book in 1549, the liturgical quest of Anglicanism has been to recover worship as truly *leit-ourgia*, a "work of the people," which is the root meaning of this Greek word. The most recent American Prayer Book invites us to take the next step in this movement of recovering the liturgy for all God's people, a movement begun in Archbishop Thomas Cranmer's remarkable sixteenth-century reforms, the first step in this continuing Anglican quest.

One of my assumptions for this work is that the 1979 Book of Common Prayer[1] brings to fruition some of the fondest ideals of the early reformers. Cranmer's notions about weekly celebration of eucharist as a norm for worship, for example, never took root in practice, with but rare exceptions. Morning prayer, litany, and

---

[1]Henceforth BCP 1979.

antecommunion[2] comprised the usual routine of Sunday worship until the latter part of the nineteenth century, when the weekly celebration of eucharist became more common (though nowhere universal) in the parishes.[3] BCP 1979 recovers Cranmer's assumptions about weekly communion and articulates them more clearly than any previous Prayer Book, making the implementation more practical. Now, nearly everywhere in the Episcopal Church, people have agreed that the chief act of worship on Sunday will be the celebration of the eucharist. This widespread consensus of practice represents not only something entirely new but also a reasonable progression from our origins. The practice is thoroughly Anglican.

Another assumption in this work is that the Anglican tradition in worship often suggests paths for finding creativity through controversy. Let us admit that the history of Prayer Book worship has brought alternating waves of accommodation and serious conflict, showing Anglicans as a contentious lot from time to time. Riots broke out in Cornwall and Devon after the introduction of BCP 1549. One of the numerous causes of the English Civil War in the 1640s was the introduction of the ill-fated Scottish Prayer Book of 1637. Physical violence, thankfully, has seldom typified liturgical

---

[2]Antecommunion adapts the Prayer Book communion service to omit the liturgy of the table. Thus this form of the liturgy, so common in historic Anglican usage, has no eucharistic prayer or communion of the people, since the service concludes with the liturgy of the word. See BCP 1979, 331, 359, 406–7 for the details describing such a service.

[3]Meanwhile, Cranmer's remarkable synthesis of morning prayer-litany-eucharist (or Antecommunion, as was more common) came to an end in the American tradition with BCP 1892, which allowed for shorter services, a pastoral response to the needs of an increasingly busy, urban, and industrialized people. That revision of the Prayer Book allowed a parish an alternative to Cranmer's synthesis; they could choose either morning prayer or eucharist (or antecommunion) to provide the usual pattern for Sunday worship. No longer did Episcopalians have to choose both.

conflict in Anglicanism, despite these early examples. Still, the conflicts have not been without serious theological and personal rancor. Thus we see Richard Hooker's monumental work, *Of the Laws of Ecclesiastical Polity*,[4] answering the puritan rancor against the Elizabethan settlement and the settlement's liturgical expression in BCP 1559. Ironically, the settlement undertaken by Elizabeth, a firm compromise seeking to make it possible for the English church to be both catholic and reformed, gave little satisfaction to those who thought it went either too far, on the one hand, or not far enough, on the other. Those who argued that the settlement lacked the appropriate fervor for reformation (the puritans) spoke most loudly and contentiously against it. But out of this acrimony came the most sublime of Anglican arguments in favor of Prayer Book worship, Hooker's Book 5 of *Ecclesiastical Polity*.

Other turning points in worship—the non-juring controversies,[5] the work of the evangelicals John and Charles Wesley, the

---

[4]The most readily available edition is: Richard Hooker, *Of the Laws of Ecclesiastical Polity*, 2 vol. (New York: Everyman's Library, 1907, 1963).

[5]The first non-jurors were those priests and bishops who in 1688 refused to swear allegiance to the new English monarchs, William and Mary, since they felt themselves bound by their previous oath to James II, who though in exile and no longer in power, was still alive. The terms "non-juring" and "non-jurors" refers to the fact that these priests and bishops, still ordained, lacked "jurisdiction," over a parish (for priests) or a diocese (for bishops) in the Church of England. A second and similar (though less widespread) non-juring crisis occurred with the death of Queen Anne and the accession of George I, from the German house of Hanover; non-jurors who had sworn allegiance to the house of Orange, Anne's royal house, had scruples about swearing allegiance to this new royal lineage. Non-juring bishops also ministered in the Episcopal Church in Scotland, where the Presbyterian Church was established and thus the only church with legal jurisdiction. The non-jurors, with a high regard for the monarchy, also had a high regard for the church. These were not separate issues, in their mind. They saw a fundamental linkage between high-church ideals and monarchy. The non-jurors also explored deeply into the meaning of the church's catholicity. Their liturgies often rearranged Cranmerian Prayer Book language in most non-

freedom of the American church after the Revolution and its subsequent divergent liturgical tradition (that is, divergent from the English tradition), the controversies surrounding the ritualist movement in the nineteenth century, to name but a few—have come through conflict. All this is to say that conflict is no anomaly in our tradition; in some ways it is our very lifeblood. At times Anglicans have bungled their way through the conflict. Was it necessary, for example, to imprison non-jurors in the seventeenth century or ritualists in the nineteenth? Conflict, nonetheless, forms a part of the Anglican ethos. We hammer out what is important to us through conversation-become-controversy. Without allowing it to become oppressive or violent, abusive or hurtful, we can learn from the tension. And we should not be surprised when controversy comes our way in the wake of liturgical change—or through a refusal to change.

The tradition of Anglican worship, shaped as it is by such conflict and change, brings forward to us a substantive, dynamic, never static core of practice. Accordingly, a faithful response to this living tradition shies away from dogged mimicry of the past. Thus, for example, attempts to imitate BCP 1549, its style, its rubrical demands, and its ethos, would lead us astray. No single moment in the tradition constitutes the norm for Anglicans, and we do harm to our identity and vocation if we romanticize any such moment and try to recapture it. Perhaps the catholic renewal in nineteenth-century Anglicanism,[6] with all the gifts it brought to

---

Cranmerian ways to give expression to their very catholic ideas. Drawing on Eastern sources in particular, the non-jurors brought unexpected liturgical creativity to their age, though the non-jurors flirted with outright schism with their attitudes and actions toward the established church.

[6] A movement whose first wave is often also known as the tractarian movement, after the series of tracts published to define the ideals for catholic expression in Anglicanism. The movement had its beginning with a pivotal sermon preached

the tradition, erred most clearly in its sometimes exaggerated attempts to recapture the practices of the late medieval era, a normative period for the so-called ritualists. Their looking back to this period made them miss the mark in two regards. First, the ritualists assumed a static rather than dynamic norm for the liturgy. "If the medieval catholic church did it this way, then we should do it also." One immediately wonders, why this period and not another? This question brings us to the second point. The ritualists typically failed in their attempts to bring forward authentic medieval practices; rather, they often formed their liturgy around what they *thought* the church did in the middle ages. Their thinking about the middle ages derived from the spirit of their own age, the age of romanticism. And their liturgies often tell us more about the aspirations of nineteenth-century England than about the late medieval church. The ritualists frequently had more in common with Sir Walter Scott and his Waverly novels than with actual liturgical practices in English cathedrals during the middle ages. They *thought* they were recovering these latter ideals.

The tractarian movement and its successors forced a major turning point in the Anglican tradition of worship. Anyone who worships in a parish where there are eucharistic vestments, candles on the altar, a vested choir, acolytes, and weekly eucharist must

---

in Oxford by John Keble in 1833, and the tracts followed thereafter in the 1830s and 1840s. Along with Keble, the leaders of the movement were Edward Bouverie Pusey and John Henry Newman. Newman would later leave the Church of England to convert to Roman Catholicism and subsequently become a cardinal in that church. This early wave of catholic renewal is also known as the Oxford movement, since most of its leaders and proponents taught or studied at that university. The second wave of catholic renewal is often called the ritualist movement, dating from the mid-1840s. The early tractarians, intensely sacramental in outlook, had only passing concern for elaborate ritual. The ritualist movement derived a rich and sometimes esoteric ceremonial from the sacramental ideals of the tractarians.

acknowledge a heritage from the tractarians. In the Episcopal Church, we are all heirs of the catholic renewal. I point out this misjudgment in method taken by the movements of catholic renewal in the nineteenth century to sound a warning to us, not to deride an important source of renewal for all of Anglicanism. Any time we try to freeze a moment from history and look to that moment as the norm, we miss the point of continuity and change within tradition. Tradition is a living organism, and we learn much about its current life from examining what has gone before. But the quest to recover for the present all the practices and customs of an earlier age results in something very artificial. We cannot mimic the early church, the medieval church, the Reformation church, the colonial church, the Victorian church, or the church of the BCP 1928. We cannot do that because we are the church of our age, in our cultural setting, with our knowledge about the Bible and the past, with our peculiar ways of knowing and our limitations. We cannot pretend that we are the Reformation church, fighting the battles fought then. We have our own battles to fight. Mimicry of the past may make the church look like those bands of middle-class folk who dress up in Union or Confederate uniforms on weekends and "reenact" battles. Such action might be quaint or interesting or even commendable to those who delight in all the details. The ability to re-enact, however, is not the quest of history, nor is it the passion of a living tradition. Such a tradition lives to empower people to act in their own age, not to recapture a fleeting moment from the past. Jaroslav Pelikan writes eloquently: "Tradition is the living faith of the dead; traditionalism is the dead faith of the living."[7]

---

[7]Jaroslav Pelikan, *The Emergence of the Catholic Tradition*, vol. 1 of *The Christian Tradition: A History of the Development of Doctrine* (Chicago: University of Chicago Press, 1971), 9.

The Anglican tradition hands over to us riches of great substance, and we rightly treasure these riches. But even more, the Anglican tradition shows us a method, an approach to living the liturgy. BCP 1549 may seem foreign to us, distant, almost in another language, especially if we read it in an edition preserving the archaic ways of spelling familiar words. Yet even this odd book (odd, that is, to moderns) sets forth principles that continue as hallmarks of our way of Christian worship and life: worship in the vernacular; a book for priest and people, not just priest; word *and* sacrament; simplicity, directness, plain speaking wherever possible; worship as a source for learning how to be Christian; continuity with the past shaped to meet current needs. These broad principles more than the details provide insights necessary for shaping Anglican liturgy in our own day. If we study the early Prayer Book tradition closely, we will also find further hints of a methodology to inform our current needs and practices. One example has to do with an approach to the resources of Christian antiquity, as Thomas Cranmer writes in the preface to the first Book of Common Prayer 1549, a preface included in the section called "Historical Documents" in BCP 1979:

> There was neuer anything by the wit of man so well deuised, or so surely established which (in continuace of time) hath not been corrupted: as (emong other thinges) it may plainly appere by the common prayers in the Churche, commonly called diuine seruice: the firste originall and grounde whereof, if a manne woulde search out by the auncient fathers, he shall finde that the same was not ordeyned, but of a good purpose, and for a great aduancement of godliness.[8]

Cranmer sets forth in this first substantive paragraph in his first Prayer Book what would become a crucial approach in the Prayer

---

[8]In F. E. Brightman, ed., *The English Rite: Being a Synopsis of the Sources and Revisions of the Book of Common Prayer*, 2 vols. (London: Rivingtons, 1915) 1:34. Cf. BCP 1979, 866, for modernized spelling.

Book tradition—the need to "searche out by the auncient fathers." But Cranmer cites the ancients not for the sake of mimicry but that he might join his purpose to theirs, that is, that he might ordain the liturgy for "good purpose" and especially for "a great aduancement of godliness." And indeed, Cranmer did draw on sources from antiquity, insofar as they were available to him, but his quest was for the liveliness of the church in England, not for a point-by-point correspondence to the practices of the ancients.

Following the same approach, we might look to the ancients for insights around a crucial and timely issue such as the renewal of the rites of baptism. The ancients (Justin, Tertullian, Hippolytus, Cyril, Ambrose, and many others) write about a means of Christian formation called the catechumenate, a lengthy and complex process leading to baptism. Hippolytus in particular assumes a catechumenate lasting perhaps three years, and the movement of the process effectively sets the believer apart—radically apart—from the surrounding and increasingly hostile world of the Roman empire in about the year 215. We, perhaps sensing a culture growing less hospitable to Christian living, might look to Hippolytus and the others for insights about living through such times. But in our cultural setting, it might not be appropriate to insist on a process culminating in a radical setting-apart from the world. An assumption about a three-year period for the process of formation might also be misplaced in the contemporary setting. Similarly, post-baptismal sermons of the sort preached by Cyril and Ambrose—ponderous, lengthy, and high-flown in rhetoric—would sound odd, if not boring, in twentieth-century America. Nonetheless, the ancients' general approach may suggest a template for our needs in "a great aduancement of godliness." Perhaps there is, from Hippolytus, the possibility of a serious and profound liturgical progression culminating in baptism; perhaps, from Cyril and Ambrose, there is a template for substantive post-baptismal formation of some sort. A three-year process and lofty rhetorical flourishes do not meet the needs of the church now. But perhaps the methodology does, and it is the methodology that has been adapted pastorally in the catechumenal processes available to us in *The Book of Occasional Services*.[9]

Purpose and Sources

The purpose in writing this work is two-fold. My first design is to ferret out and describe broad principles from the Anglican tradition that might enliven ordinary parish worship in the Episcopal Church today. The second, related to the first, is to provide for planners (clergy, musicians, and members of worship committees) an introduction to the peculiarly Anglican tradition from which their decisions about the liturgy must arise. I do not intend to list answers from the tradition, as if to suggest simplistically that there is a "right" way and a "wrong" way, but I hope that a basic familiarity with the Anglican heritage will help planners know the various options before them and (most important) the necessary questions to ask. Three sources inform this endeavor. The first and most important is the most recent Prayer Book, BCP 1979. This book provides a liturgical norm for the Episcopal Church in the United States of America.[10] Yet this norm itself is evolving, leaning toward a next Book of Common Prayer. And if we continue in the Anglican heritage, we must assume that there will be a next one. The preface to BCP 1662 reads:

> The particular Forms of divine Worship, and the Rites and Ceremonies appointed to be vsed therein, being things in their own nature indifferent, and alterable, and so acknowledged: it is but reasonable that vpon waighty

---

[9] *The Book of Occasional Services: 1994* (New York: Church Hymnal Corporation, 1995), 114ff.

[10] Henceforth ECUSA.

and important considerations, according to the various exigency of times and occasions, such changes and alterations should be made therein as to those that are in place of Authority, should from time to time seem either necessary or expedient.[11]

BCP 1979 is a thoroughly Anglican book. Its departure from Cranmerian language in Rite II in no way undercuts this Anglican identity. This book represents but the most recent distillation of the very ideals held dear by Cranmer and the other reformers. The practices of BCP 1979 define the norm for the Episcopal Church, for the book represents a consensus for the time being wrought through controversy. New controversies no doubt will test the margins of the current book and require a new consensus. But for now, BCP 1979 gives the Episcopal Church the definitive core for its worship. The Prayer Book, then, deserves our respect (although not our undying allegiance, which becomes uncomfortably akin to idolatry) not simply because of its liturgical merit, rich in its own right, but most of all because respect to the Prayer Book becomes a way of respecting brothers and sisters whose consensus and assent the Prayer Book represents. In reality, it is not the Prayer Book to which we owe respect; instead, our respect is rightly directed toward the larger community, the Episcopal Church, from which the Prayer Book takes its current expression.

A second procession of sources comes in the historic Prayer Books, from 1549 to 1928. These books—in their similarities and differences and (especially) in a deeper underlying purpose that cuts across the entire history of Anglican worship—inform our understanding of the Anglican way. The structures of meaning from the Prayer Book tradition give us a provisional norm, always accountable to the current Prayer Book and its expressions.

A third source derives from historic Anglicanism in general and

---

[11]In Brightman, *English Rite*, 1:27. The irony, of course, is that at least by force of law BCP 1662 remains the current Prayer Book of the Church of England.

especially the writings of the reformers. And since the English reformation was long and hard-fought, effectively stretching from 1529 (Henry VIII's first movement to repudiate the authority of Rome) to 1688 (the Glorious Revolution, with the accession of William and Mary to the English throne), there are a lot of reformers to read and much evidence in this category. This formative era lends special insight into the vocation and identity peculiar to Anglicanism. Alternating between controversy (usually rancorous) and consensus (often tentative and fleeting), the movement of the English reformation suggests a paradigm for authentic and committed expressions of Anglican worship to this day. The various writers from the episcopal end of the spectrum, as opposed to those on the puritan-presbyterian-congregationalist end, give a classical expression to the Anglican way of being Christian. On balance, the episcopal end of the spectrum bore a greater influence in shaping the Anglican way, but it was a *moderated* episcopal influence, having been shaped through one hundred fifty years of conflict and conversation with the puritans and others. That expression evolved through the rhythms of controversy and consensus—and it evolves still.

Let us return to the issue of aesthetic, for Episcopalians invest much energy pursuing ideals of beauty as they deal with worship. I suspect that we waste much energy and in fact often enervate ourselves in the process. Accordingly, this work focuses not on issues of aesthetic but on issues of vocation and identity in worship: Who are we? Where do we come from? What are we called to do and to be as we gather as a worshiping community? What are we called to become? Do we as Anglicans have a distinctive calling among the various Christian communions? I do not set out to answer every question, at least not in a point-by-point fashion, but these questions of vocation and identity point the way for my twofold purpose, described at the head of this section. Despite the problematic distractions into which aesthetic issues often draw us, I am nonetheless unwilling to abandon entirely the conversation around these issues. Aidan Kavanagh, for one, argues convincingly that liturgy forces the question of taste, that the language of aesthetic, even in our post-modern time, need not be merely a private language, and that in fact it is possible and necessary to recover a public, communal language of aesthetic.[12] One purpose of this book is to suggest, ever so tentatively, such a language. My assumptions, however, move from vocation and identity to aesthetic, not the other way around. The Anglican vocation and identity give Anglican worship a particular aesthetic. Too often, I fear, we allow Anglican worship to become a hodgepodge of quandaries about taste, a hodgepodge sprung loose from considerations of who we are.

The reformers usually described matters of ceremonial (an issue of aesthetic) under the term *adiaphora*, meaning "non-essentials" or "matters of indifference." Having so described them as concerns of secondary importance, they proceeded to argue a lengthy case for freedom around such issues.[13] Here marks the often tenuous balance for Anglican worship, one that keeps aesthetic in perspective as a secondary concern yet all the while forswears the lackadaisical attitudes that would have us shrug the shoulders in boredom. The *adiaphora*, unchecked, can overwhelm the liturgy, and thus they warrant our concern. We cannot afford to ignore them, lest our acts of worship become strings of one non-essential after another. We need to know what is important and what is not. We need to distinguish between primary and secondary concerns. As Anglicans, we need to maintain a sense of liberty around the

---

[12]Aidan Kavanagh, *Elements of Rite: A Handbook of Liturgical Style* (New York: Pueblo, 1982), 82-104.

[13]See, for example, Hooker, *Ecclesiastical Polity*, 5. 4.

adiaphora, recognizing all the while their individual merits and limitations.

A description of principles, I contend, suits an Anglican approach to the liturgy quite well. Handbooks of detailed ceremonial, common in Anglicanism in the aftermath of the ritualist movement,[14] serve a useful though limited purpose, in that they illustrate *one* way of worshiping God. Often, however, they major in the *adiaphora* and make absolute what would in ordinary Anglican parlance remain a matter of freedom. Their remarkable precision and passion for detail, alas, do not take into account the great diversity of architectural settings for worship. What works in one building simply might not fit in another. More importantly, these handbooks do little to honor the heritage and makeup of a particular worshiping community. I know of a parish that had a hundred-year heritage of what used to be called "low church" worship—morning prayer three Sundays each month with eucharist on the fourth. Then the parish called a rector who immediately on arrival instituted daily "mass" according to the rite in *The Anglican Missal*,[15] along with all the "high church" and anglo-

---

[14]See, for example, *Ritual Notes on the Order of Divine Service*, 5th ed. (London: William Walker, 1907); Percy Dearmer, *The Parson's Handbook*, 12th ed. (London: Oxford University Press, 1932; 1st ed., 1899); and Dennis G. Michno, *A Priest's Handbook: The Ceremonies of the Church* (Wilton, CT: Morehouse-Barlow, 1983).

[15]See, for example, *The Anglican Missal* (London: The Society of Ss. Peter and Paul, 1921). There is no one definitive missal, since several versions, each claiming its own merit, circulate through the Anglican communion. The various missals, none of which has ever found official church sanction, attempt to reorder the Prayer Book eucharist along the lines of the Roman Catholic mass. Popular in some anglo-catholic circles, these books superimpose a pre-Vatican II ideal of the Roman mass, complete with all the ceremonial details, onto the Prayer Book rite. A few bishops have supported the missals, others have tolerated them, turning a blind eye, while others still have sought to ban their use entirely.

catholic trappings. The restrained ceremonial to which the people were accustomed gave way to the exuberance of catholic Anglicanism. The priest, well-intentioned, merely followed all the details of *Ritual Notes* and the rubrics of the Missal. You can imagine the turbulence that ensued.

A book of broadly stated principles, I believe, can avoid these limitations. And so this work does not pretend to be a book of ceremonial, although ceremonial remains one of its concerns. An understanding of these principles will enable wise ceremonial choices. The hope is that these basic ideas about Anglican worship will help priests and parishes, in their locale, with their building, with their particular community of baptized Christians, make careful choices about the timeless celebrations of word and sacrament. The shape of this book requires that priest and people enter the conversation, for if much is said here, much is left unspoken.

A First Principle: Simplicity

The title of this work offers a rudimentary principle to explain the Prayer Book approach to liturgy. A sensibility of *admirable simplicity* or *uncomplicated solemnity* best describes the Anglican way of worship. The Prayer Books assume a straightforward approach from priest and people, leaving bare the powerful word and life-giving sacraments. The Prayer Books invite the worshiper to trust God and God's gifts; excessive adornment becomes superfluous in this ethos of worship, for word and sacrament provide their own adornment. Ceremonial does not add to the adornment. Appropriately chosen, ceremonial merely points toward the gifts. Excessive ceremonial, on the other hand, obscures the view. The sixteenth-century reformation of the liturgy came most of all as a paring-down, not an adding-on. (Will not any effort at liturgical renewal involve at least some of this approach?) The first Prayer

Book (1549) includes a section entitled, "Of Ceremonies: Why Some Be Abolished and Some Retayned." It begins:

> Of such Ceremonies as be vsed in the Churche, and haue had their begin-nyng by the institucion of man: Some at the first were of godly intent and purpose deuised, and yet at length turned to vanitie and superstitiō: Some entred into the Church by vndiscrete deuocion, and suche a zeale as was without knowleage: and for-because they were winked at in the beginning, they grewe dayly to more and more abuses, which not onely for their vnprofitableness, but also because they haue much blynded the people, and obscured the glory of God, are worthy to be cut awaye, and cleane reiected. Other there be, whiche alghouth they haue been deuised by man: yet it is thought good to reserue them still, as well for a decent ordre in the Churche (for the whiche they were first deuised) as because they pertayne to edificacion: wherunto all thinges doen in the Churche (as the Apostle teacheth) ought to be referred.[16]

Thus I argue for simplicity and directness in the liturgical celebrations, for herein lies the solemnity. At the eucharist, the actions, gestures, music, and postures should all point toward bread broken and wine poured out. The breadth of Anglican practice welcomes both modesty and extravagance in what is done around the bread and wine. Both approaches can appropriately point toward God's gifts for God's people. Some, however, confuse a pedestrian approach, spur-of-the-moment planning, or ceremonial sloppiness for modesty. Without a judicious and thoughtful approach to the celebration, even if that approach is restrained, the essentials of bread and wine may be obscured in the confusion. On the other hand, excessive ceremonial may suggest to the worshiping community that the numerous signs of the cross and genuflections are more important than taking bread and wine, blessing them, breaking the bread and pouring out the wine, so that the gifts might be shared in communion.

---

[16]Brightman, *English Rite*, 1:38–40. The text alludes to Romans 10 and 1 Corinthians 14.

The sensibility shaping this book tends toward an aesthetic of simplicity, with the understanding that less is often in fact more. Simplicity can take shape in a variety of styles. I can find no single ceremonial or aesthetic norm (outside the Prayer Book rubrics) for Anglican liturgy. Simplicity can find appropriate expression in grand style. Some of the most authentically straightforward and accessible liturgies I have known have been celebrated in the anglo-catholic tradition, with all its measured exuberance. The exuberance does not have to result in clutter, for careful anglo-catholic liturgy will point toward the riches at the center of the celebration. Unthinking exuberance, however, will obscure these riches. This book takes a bias against busy-ness, ceremonial clutter, unnecessary accretions, and confusing or gratuitous gestures. No single aesthetic style has the franchise on ceremonial propriety. And every style, degraded, can make the liturgy into a collecting ground for meaningless clutter and excess.

The rest of this book has as its concern the practical working-out of Anglican liturgy and this first principle in the parish setting, and it deals with the services in the order they come in BCP 1979. Chapter Two thus outlines the principles surrounding the daily office. Chapter Three addresses the rites of initiation (baptism and confirmation); Chapter Four, the eucharist; and Chapter Five, the pastoral offices (including marriage, ministration to the sick, and burial). Chapter Six, a conclusion, will suggest some strategies for planning the liturgy in a parish as well as the place of a worship committee in that work.

But some additional principles of a general nature apply to the liturgies discussed in the succeeding chapters, and these principles form the necessary completion to this introduction.

Word and Sacrament

The reformers intended a recovery of both word and sacrament in worship. They did not play the one off against the other but instead saw the one as the necessary complement of the other. BCP 1549 described a daily (and public) celebration of word, rich in its presentation of scripture and psalmody.[17] The Sunday and holy day celebration offered an even richer fare of word, with morning prayer, the litany, and the communion service (at least that part constituting the liturgy of the word, even on the occasions when the liturgy of the table was not celebrated). Cranmer's ideal was to make weekly, participatory eucharist the norm for the English church. And although his norm never extended into common practice, the *symbol* of that norm remained intact through the weekly celebration of the liturgy of the word belonging to the eucharist. Even when the sacrament was celebrated with varying degrees of frequency, the reformers never sought to understand word without its completion in sacrament, nor did they isolate sacrament from its context in word. The one found its complement in the other.[18]

The puritan faction among the reformers, challenging a more moderate mainstream of reform, steadfastly emphasized the reading of scripture and especially its use as a resource for preaching. In fact, they often used the phrase "God's word" to refer to the act of preaching alone, much to the chagrin of Richard Hooker, the definitive theologian of the Prayer Book settlement of the late

---

[17]BCP 1552, while still assuming a public rite for morning prayer and evening prayer, erodes this assumption by allowing clergy to fulfill their *personal* obligation to the daily office by praying it either publicly or privately. BCP 1549 assumes that the cleric's personal obligation to pray daily will be fulfilled only in the public setting. Brightman, *English Rite*, 1:38–39, 127.

[18]Hooker, *Ecclesiastical Polity*, 5. 1. 2–3.

sixteenth century. Hooker saw the limitation of God's word to sermons alone as far too narrow.[19] While the English reformation always provided a place for preaching and held in esteem its importance through the various official *Books of Homilies*,[20] moderate reformers like Hooker expressed a willingness to let scripture speak for itself on regular occasion. The daily offices, for example, provided lengthy readings from scripture without noting a place for a sermon—to the irritation of the puritans.[21]

BCP 1979, reflecting the recovery of liturgical preaching in our time, is the first Prayer Book specifically to provide for the option of preaching at the daily office.[22] BCP 1979 also restores a rich liturgy of the word to the eucharist, providing for the first time the norm of three readings (usually including a lection from the Hebrew scriptures), psalmody, and choices among canticles. Note that the Prayer Book marks the place for the sermon in bold print and makes no mention of its being an option.[23] Daily liturgy of the

---

[19] Hooker, *Ecclesiastical Polity*, 5. 21. 2. and 5. 22. 12.

[20] The English Church first arrived at the idea of publishing a collection of prescribed homilies in 1542. Such a book, church leaders argued, would provide a resource for communicating the riches of the word especially in parishes served by unlearned clergy. The first *Book of Homilies* was published in 1547, with a second volume in 1571. Article XXXV of the Articles of Religion lists by title the twenty-one homilies from the second *Book of Homilies*. See BCP 1979, 874–75.

[21] Horton Davies, *Worship and Theology in England*, 5 vol. (Princeton, NJ: Princeton University Press, 1965) 2:138.

[22] BCP 1979, 142. Although preaching was customary at morning prayer or evening prayer in earlier Prayer Books, especially at the Sunday service, the rubrics actually made no place for it. The sermon came after the creed at the eucharist, in the office-litany-communion order in place until 1892. Paul V. Marshall, *Prayer Book Parallels*, 2 vols. (New York: Church Hymnal Corporation, 1989, 1990), 1:330–31.

[23] BCP 1979, 326, 358. Earlier Prayer Books noted in the rubrics a place for the sermon after the creed. BCP 1549 set the pattern: "After the Crede ended, shall follwe the Sermon or Homely, or some portion of one of the Homelyes, as thei

word is the norm for this Prayer Book, as is the word-rich celebration of sacrament for Sunday and other major holy days. Word and sacrament belong together in our Prayer Book practice. There is no option to choose between the two.

The Peculiarities of the Rubrics

Three rules (and very important ones they are) prevail in the rubrical language of the Prayer Books.[24] First, when the rubrics offer choices, the first choice has the presumption of favor. Thus, for example, in BCP 1979, Rite II rubrics describing the posture of the people during the eucharistic prayer read, "The people stand or kneel." Standing is preferred, but kneeling is an option. For Rite I, on the other hand, the rubrics read, "The people kneel or stand."[25] Here, kneeling is the preferred posture, with standing an option. Liturgical settings with different ritual language may bring with them different presumptions about posture, according to these rubrics. In both cases the presumption is not definitive, so an alternative is allowed. Priests and worship committees need to know how to read such rubrics and how to make sense of them, considering the needs in the communities they serve.

Second, the rubrics speak clearly and precisely in using "should" and "may." The rubric at the beginning of both eucha-

---

shabe herafter deuided." Brightman, *English Rite*, 2:648.

[24] The rubrics are the directions for the various services in the Prayer Book. By the late middle ages, it became customary in the various service books to print these instructions in red to distinguish them from the words to be said for the service. (Hence the term rubric, deriving from the Latin *rubeus*—the same root word for ruby.) Another convention is to print the rubrics either in italics or another distinctive typeface to set these liturgical directions apart from the words of the rite.

[25] BCP 1979, 362, 334.

ristic rites reads, "A hymn, psalm, or anthem *may* be sung."[26] Thus the rubrics allow but do not require an opening hymn. In the section entitled "Concerning the Celebration," rubrics about the deacon's liturgical role begin, "A deacon *should* read the Gospel and *may* lead the Prayers of the People."[27] The presumption about the role of gospel-lector falls in favor of a deacon (rather than a priest) if a deacon is present in the liturgy. This presumption is stronger than the option suggested in rubrics with the word "may" but falls short of an absolute requirement. The same rubrics also allow but do not require a deacon to lead the intercessions; the force of presumption in the deacon's role as gospel-lector is missing at this point.

Third, rubrics other than those discussed in points one and two are descriptive, not proscriptive. Rubrics describe; they do not prohibit.[28] If the rubrics state, "The people sit," then they sit. But rubrical force is very precise on this point. If the rubrics do *not* describe an action, then the action does not belong in the rite. A good example has to do with music before and after a service, as dealt with in BCP 1892 and BCP 1928, where the rubric entitled "Hymns and Anthems" reads:

> Hymns set forth and allowed by the authority of this Church, and Anthems in the words of Holy Scripture or of the Book of Common Prayer, may be

---

[26]Ibid., 323, 255. Emphasis added.

[27]Ibid., 322, 354. Emphasis added.

[28]The one exception I am aware of comes from BCP 1549, where the rubric pertaining to the institution narrative (the part of the eucharistic prayer describing Jesus' words and actions with bread and wine at the Last Supper) reads, "These wordes before rehersed are to be saied, turning still to the Altar, *without any eleuacion, or shewing the Sacrament to the people.*" (emphasis added). This rubric, prohibiting an action from the Roman rite held in disrepute by the reformers, gives us the sole exception proving the rule. See Brightman, *English Rite*, 2:694.

sung before and after any Office in this Book, and also before and after Sermons.[29]

The absence of this general rubric in BCP 1979 means something. Thus if a particular service allows a hymn, psalm, or anthem before or afterward, the rubrics will say so. In fact, at every point where the rite allows or requires music, the rubrics in BCP 1979 will so state. The daily offices, however, make no mention of beginning with a hymn, psalm, or anthem. In fact, the first rubric in Rite II morning prayer reads:

> The Officiant begins the service with one or more of these sentences of Scripture, or with the versicle, "Lord, open our lips" on page 80.

The service begins, therefore, with one of the two alternatives stated, for the structure of the offices in BCP 1979 does not allow for a processional hymn.

These three rules for reading the rubrics are simple. But we can see that the rubrics bear close reading, for sometimes they say something different from what we might *think* they say or *ought* to say. What is left unsaid is especially important, and priests and worship committees should think carefully before deciding on actions that test the limits of those rubrical silences, for the rubrics shape the structure of the rites as much as do the texts themselves. They give life to the liturgy, and careless reading of the rubrics can result in the very busy-ness that obscures what is central to the act of worship.

The Prayer Book Way *as* Via Media

Richard Hooker sought to chart a course for Anglicanism between the demands of Roman Catholicism on the one hand and those of the puritans on the other. Hooker's methodology, called a "middle

---

[29]Marshall, *Prayer Book Parallels*, 1:84–85.

way" (*via media*), attempts to encompass and embrace whatever truths might be discovered from these opposing forces of catholicism and protestantism while avoiding the extremes of both. "Compromise" thus does not quite describe Hooker's intent. This middle way, so carefully described, has entered the ordinary language Anglicans use to describe their vocation and identity.

The Prayer Book models this approach. For the Prayer Book differs, on the one hand, from the puritan approach to liturgy, suggested typically in *directories* for worship. These books of worship, like the *Westminster Directory* (1644), offer outlines for worship and assume occasions for extemporaneous prayer as a norm.[30] The Prayer Book describes a precise order for service (sometimes with options) and assumes set forms for prayer.[31] On the other hand, the Prayer Book avoids the rubrical precision of the Roman Rite, especially as it found its expression in the rites emerging from the Council of Trent (1545–63). Although the Prayer Book exists precisely for the sake of uniformity in forms of worship,[32] the implementation of a uniform rite follows no strin-

---

[30]See the order for communion from the *Westminster Directory* in *Prayers of the Eucharist: Early and Reformed*, ed. R. C. D. Jasper and G. J. Cuming, 2d ed. (New York: Oxford University Press, 1980), 187–192. The tradition of the *Book of Common Order* for the Presbyterians and other free-church Christians in England derives from early reformed works like the *Westminster Directory*. See Charles Wheatly, *A Rational Illustration of the Book of Common Prayer of the Church of England* (Oxford: Oxford University Press, 1846; 1st ed., 1710), 1. 1–3., for a classical Anglican response to puritan pressures for freedom from set liturgical forms.

[31]BCP 1979 is the first Prayer Book to offer outlines of services for eucharist, marriage, and burial. See 400–5, 435–36, and 506–7. Even these outlines are set forth in such a way that they should not be taken as the norm, and the instructions for celebrating the eucharist in this manner state explicitly that such a celebration is not intended for the principal Sunday or weekly celebration of the eucharist.

[32]See the Preface to BCP 1549 in Brightman, 1:34–38.

gent rule apart from the rubrics, themselves rather concise in comparison to those in the Tridentine rites. Moreover, Anglicanism has tended to tolerate divergence from rubrical norms, whereas the Roman church has the structures for stricter enforcement. With few exceptions, the Anglican way has been to rely not on legal or canonical authority to enforce the Prayer Book rites but on the moral authority within the ordination promises of loyalty "to the doctrine, discipline, and worship of Christ as this Church has received them."[33] Persuasion and accountability to a larger community set the primary means by which Episcopalians maintain faithfulness to the Prayer Book way of worship. The liturgical renewal of the 1960s and 1970s illustrates this point. In the Episcopal Church, various books (and booklets) made their way through trial usage and much haggling to arrive at a consensus, hardfought, in a new Book of Common Prayer. *Episcopalians had to be persuaded.* As for the Roman rites coming out of Vatican II during

---

[33]BCP 1979, 526, 538; cf. 513. See also Marshall, *Prayer Book Parallels*, 1:608–9 for earlier rescensions of this phrase in the American Prayer Books and in BCP 1662. See Canon 3. 14. 1(a) (1991) for the duties of the clergy regarding worship and Canon 4. 1. 1(3) for the disciplinary canon which reads: "A Bishop, Presbyter, or Deacon of this Church shall be liable to presentment and trial for the following offenses, viz., . . . (3) Violation of the Rubrics of the Book of Common Prayer." Presentment, a rare course taken in the Episcopal Church, is rarer still for rubrical violations. The standard commentary on the canons fails to mention in its elucidation a single instance of such a trial in ECUSA. See *Annotated Constitutions and Canons for the Government of the Protestant Episcopal Church in the United States of America, Otherwise Known as the Episcopal Church*, 2 vols. (New York: The Office of General Convention, 1985), 2:970–72. The enforcement of the Prayer Book rubrics against ritualists through public trial in nineteenth-century England (and subsequent imprisonment in a few cases) proved untenable, an embarrassment both to the courts and to the church, as well as to the English public. Bishops then abandoned this means of coercing ritualists to follow the texts and rubrics of the Prayer Book. Books such as the *Anglican Missal*, based loosely on Prayer Book materials but arranged according to the books of the Roman Rite, soon followed.

these same years, the books simply showed up in the parishes and were put in use. Selling the rites to the people came afterward, but even then selling the rites was incidental, for the magisterium had decided (and decided definitively) already. For Episcopalians, selling the rites to the people had to come first.

Thus Anglicanism charts a middle way between the puritan directories and the Roman magisterium. This course has its drawbacks, some of which are evidenced in the Church of England today, where BCP 1662 remains by force of law the official Prayer Book. But various forms of the *Anglican Missal* have long found tolerance in many dioceses. And most bishops have tacitly agreed to allow the use of the proposed BCP of 1928-29, a book that received church approval but failed to pass the houses of Parliament. Then there is the *Alternative Services Book* (ASB) of 1980, a book bringing to bear the insights of recent liturgical renewal for the Church of England. Even this book, however, lacks the full authority of an official Prayer Book, for that is still BCP 1662. The Parliamentary resistance to Prayer Book revision earlier in this century contributes to a lack of liturgical uniformity in the Church of England. The English situation has probably edged the church away from the *via media* in its worship sensibilities and toward the attitudes of the directories. With so many possibilities for the parishes, consensus about worship has effectively lost its center. It is not quite laissez faire, and not quite chaos, but the situation is not at all satisfactory. Such problems do not prevail in ECUSA, but the English situation points out the possibility of failings when the center does not hold.

But the middle way of Anglicanism can enliven creativity as well as engender chaos. The light touch used in exerting external authority around the Prayer Book makes it possible for the entire church to realize emerging liturgical issues and needs. For example, the widespread tinkering with the rubrics in the 1950s and

1960s helped illustrate the need for Prayer Book revision—and helped clarify exactly what points needed revising most. The case of the non-jurors illustrates a similar point. Anglicanism has the resiliency through this middle way to incorporate the insights of those like the non-jurors for whom the center fails to hold. This not-quite-schismatic group continued in parallel existence to the Church of England for a century and a half, bringing much liturgical scholarship (and some eccentricities) to their high-church aspirations. For example, they reconstructed Cranmer's eucharistic language in a fashion akin to ancient prayers of Eastern Christianity. This work of theirs would ultimately find its way into the Scottish Episcopal Church (a non-juring body) and from there into the American Prayer Book tradition. Their work, scandalously outside the mainstream in its day, now has its place as Eucharistic Prayer 1 of Rite I in BCP 1979, the historic prayer in the American Prayer Books. Anglicanism, with its middle way, has the curious flexibility to incorporate unlikely and creative innovations.

The Sufficiency of the Prayer Book

The preface to BCP 1549 reads:

> [B]y this ordre, the curates shal nede none other bookes for their publique seruice, but this boke and the Bible: by the meanes wherof, the people shall not be at so great charge for bookes, as in tyme past they haue been.[34]

Bible and Prayer Book have provided Anglicans with the resources for worship, and the tradition mandates none besides these. The reformers had two purposes in establishing this principle. First, the multiplication of books goes hand-in-hand with increasingly complex rules. If a given service requires several books, then the

---

[34]Brightman, *English Rite*, 1:36.

rules governing that service are likely to be more confounding for minister and people. Thus the 1549 Preface reads again:

> Moreouer the nōbre and hardnes of the rules called the pie, and the manifolde chaunginges of the seruice, was the cause, yt to turne the boke onlye, was so hard and intricate a matter, than many times, there was more busines to fynd out what should be read, then to read it when it was founde out.[35]

The multiplication of books may violate the basic Anglican canon of simplicity.

A second reason for the compilation of liturgical materials into a single book derives from the reformers' concern to address the needs of the people and not just the role of the priest. The Prayer Book is a book for priest and people. It sets aside any esoteric pretense that might arise from the priest alone knowing how to work many books. The publishing of the Prayer Book debunks the secretive aspects of the priest's role, so common in the late middle ages. At the great thanksgiving, the 1549 rubrics direct the priest to "saye or syng, *playnly and distinctly*," that part of the liturgy considered heretofore the most sacrosanct and secretive, limited to the priest himself and thus to be said in a quiet voice or a whisper —the eucharistic prayer itself.[36] The course taken in the first Prayer Book follows the widespread reformation ideal of honoring the role of the laity and recovering a role for them in the liturgy as well as in the wider life of the church. The introduction of the liturgy (and the Bible) in the vernacular followed the same principle. A priest might well have known Latin, but the church's worship is not just for the priest. It is for priest and people together,

---

[35]Ibid. The "pie" was a book of rules detailing the particulars of the church calendar, especially as it affected the daily offices. By late medieval times in England, the rules and multiple layers of exceptions had grown out of control.

[36]Brightman, *English Rite*, 2:688. Emphasis added.

and the language of the people takes precedence in determining the liturgy.

Thus Anglicans have taken these vernacular volumes, Bible and Prayer Book, as indispensable guides in their practice of Christianity. Other books might supplement Bible and Prayer Book, but these two are requisite.[37] On the contemporary liturgical scene, several slim volumes supplement the materials in the Prayer Book—*The Book of Occasional Services, Lesser Feasts and Fasts,*[38] and *Supplemental Liturgical Materials.*[39] All these books have the approval of General Convention; none of them, however, has the binding authority of the Prayer Book. Some of the materials in these books may represent the movement toward a new and emerging liturgical consensus in the Episcopal Church, and they will likely help shape the next American Prayer Book. Now, however, they remain options—helpful and suitable options, in many cases—but options nonetheless. Liturgically, the Prayer Book is sufficient. It alone is necessary.

An Ethos of Reform and Revision

The Episcopal Church claims a total of nine Prayer Books in its heritage: the English books of 1549, 1552, 1559, 1604, and 1662, and the American books of 1789, 1892, 1928, and 1979. Add to these the various Prayer Book revisions in the Anglican provinces world-

---

[37]See Article VI in the Articles of Religion, Of the Sufficiency of Scripture: "Holy Scripture containeth all things necessary to salvation: so that whatsoever is not read therein, nor may be proved thereby, is not to be required of any man, that it should be believed as an article of the Faith, or be thought requisite or necessary to salvation." BCP 1979, 868. Cf. Hooker, *Ecclesiastical Polity*, 2. 8. 7.

[38]*Lesser Feasts and Fasts: 1994* (New York: Church Hymnal Corporation, 1995).

[39]*Supplemental Liturgical Materials* (New York: Church Hymnal Corporation, 1991).

wide: South Africa, New Zealand, Canada, Australia, and all the rest. Add to these the experiments of the non-jurors in the seventeenth and eighteenth centuries and the tractarians in the nineteenth and twentieth—books in the Prayer Book tradition lacking official sanction but influential in their various spheres. The evidence is overwhelming: reform and revision mark the way for Anglican liturgy.

There is a caveat, however. Until the mid-point of the present century, Prayer Book reform mostly involved rearranging Cranmerian language. Syntax, phrases, whole chunks of material would remain the same before and after revision. The revisers would simply arrange the units of the liturgy, these reasonably stable aspects of the tradition, according to the needs of the day. The clearest evidence of this trend comes in the eucharistic rites. Take, for example, this section from BCP 1552:

> O Lord and heauenly father, we thy humble seruaunts entierly desire thy fatherly goodnes, mercifully to accept this our Sacrifice of prayse and thanks geuing: most humbly beseching thee to graunt, that by the merites and death of thy sonne Jesus Christe, and through fayth in his bloud, we and al thy whole church may obtayne remission of oure synnes, and all other benefytes of his Passion. And here we offre and presente unto thee, O lord, our selfes, our soules, and bodies, to be a reasonable, holy, and liuely Sacrifice unto thee: humbly beseching thee, that al we which be partakers of this holy Communion, maye bee fulfylled with thy grace and heauenly benediccion. And although we bee unworthy throughe oure manifolde sinnes to offre unto thee any Sacrifice: yet we beseche thee to accept this our bounden duetie and seruice, not weighing our merites, but pardoning our offences, through Jesus Christ our Lord; by whom and with whom, in the unitie of the holy ghost, all honour and glory bee unto thee, O father almightie, world without ende. Amen.[40]

These phrases sound familiar to Episcopalians, for they have made their way into the eucharistic prayers of the American books, in-

---

[40]Brightman, *English Rite*, 2:707–9.

cluding BCP 1979. Prayer 1 of Rite I, the historic American eucharistic prayer, preserves this language, changing only those words and phrases whose archaic usage clearly obscures the meaning. Thus we now offer a "living sacrifice" rather than a "liuely Sacrifice," to cite one example. Episcopalians might be surprised, however, to know that in BCP 1552 this prayer comes *after* communion. It is not a part of the eucharist prayer; it is instead a post-communion prayer. The English Prayer Books through 1662 (remember, the current book) follow this same pattern. Even the *Alternative Services Book* of 1980 provides for this usage among its various options. The American books, however, follow the patterns developed through the liturgical tinkerings of the non-jurors, specifically those in Scotland. The non-jurors rearranged these Cranmerian materials to follow the patterns of some of the classical eucharistic prayers of Eastern Orthodoxy. They changed the words very little; they only moved the furniture to reflect what they considered a richer eucharistic theology clarifying Christ's presence in the eating and drinking.

Actually, BCP 1552 itself represents a shift from BCP 1549, where the material in question also comes in the eucharistic prayer. But even the 1549 prayer is an odd amalgam, a fitting-together of stuff from the familiar prayer of the medieval Roman rite within a quasi-Eastern structure—with elements from German Protestant sources thrown in for good measure. The vague (and Protestant) eucharistic theology Cranmer intended in this prayer did not come through. Thus many people failed to understand the prayer in terms of eucharistic memorial as Cranmer had hoped. Some, like the catholic-minded bishop Stephen Gardiner, seemed intentionally to misunderstand the prayer in terms of a higher eucharistic theology, one clearly suggesting Christ's presence, and not a memorial. So Cranmer, in the revisions leading up to BCP 1552, took steps to rectify these misunderstandings. Saving this problematic prayer until after communion solved his problem. Having the priest praying these words over the people conveys something entirely different from his praying them over the bread and wine.

Such convoluted—and maddening—rearrangements typified Prayer Book revision until about the middle of the twentieth century. At that time, scholarly studies of ancient liturgical sources discovered late in the previous century converged with a popular yearning for liturgical renewal. This popular movement arose first in Roman Catholic circles but quickly spread to isolated parishes through the Anglican communion, gaining strength all the while.[41] Recognizing the need for more drastic Prayer Book revision, the bishops of the Anglican communion, meeting at Lambeth Palace in 1958, called for the work that resulted in such books as our own BCP 1979 and the Church of England's *Alternative Services Book* 1980. These books and others like them have gone beyond the customary moving around of Cranmerian furniture seen in earlier revisions. The new books have raided the riches of the ancient church and the Anglican tradition to meet the needs of a worshiping church in the modern world. Anglicans thus have continued the course of revision, already ingrained in our ethos. Widespread revision, incited by this new familiarity with the ancients and motivated by a popular desire for a life of worship, has taken hold. Cranmer, possessing an imagination sparked by what he knew from the scriptures and the ancient Christian writers, took a similar course in his own day. His resources from the ancients were limited. Ours, thankfully, are over-brimming.

---

[41]See Gregory Dix, *The Shape of the Liturgy* (London: Dacre Press, 1945) and A. G. Hebert, ed., *The Parish Communion* (London: SPCK, 1937) for two wellheads of influence on the Anglican scene—Dix in the scholarly realm, Hebert in the popular movement.

Architecture and Worship: The Crucial Link

The buildings Christians worship in shape their manner of worship. And often when Christians desire to reshape the liturgy, they look to changes in church architecture for primary strategies. This principle holds true for the church throughout history. Perhaps the most dramatic shift in the liturgy came in the fourth century, when Christianity, no longer an illicit religion in the Roman empire, gradually left the house church (with associations of intimacy and discipline) for the huge public auditorium called the basilica (with associations of splendor and acculturation). Vast cultural changes affecting the liturgy coincided with these architectural changes. The ceremonial style that fit in the context of the more intimate gathering proved woefully understated in the basilica, where there might be a crowd numbering in the thousands. These changes—architectural, cultural, and liturgical— were so tightly intertwined, in fact, that one cannot be separated from the others.

G. W. O. Addleshaw's classic work, *The Architectural Setting of Anglican Worship*,[42] describes the interplay of liturgy and architecture (including the various accoutrements and church furnishings) as it has been played out in our tradition. At times the setting for the liturgy has reflected more clearly the ideals of liturgical reform in a given era than has the Prayer Book. For example, people worshiped according to the rites of BCP 1662 during two vastly different and revolutionary eras of architectural innovation—the middle and late seventeenth century, and the middle and late nineteenth century. Inigo Jones and Christopher Wren

---

[42]G. W. O. Addleshaw, *The Architectural Setting of Anglican Worship: An Inquiry into the Arrangements for Public Worship in the Church of England from the Reformation to the Present Day* (London: Faber and Faber, 1948). No church building committee should proceed without reading this work.

influenced the earlier era with ideals of simplicity within their church buildings (some of which were huge, seating two thousand or more). Their works put every worshiper as close as possible to the liturgical action and emphasized the auditory aspects of the holy. That is, everyone should *hear* the word and thereby be drawn closer to the divine. Such were the aspirations of architecture (and liturgy) in an age beginning to be drawn to ideals of enlightenment and rationality, an era fascinated with possibilities of words and logical discourse. The Cambridge Camden Society, on the other hand, led by John Mason Neale and Benjamin Webb, developed a distinctively new architecture in the nineteenth century. Their approach, in keeping with the catholic idealism of the tractarian movement, focused on the beauty of holiness in the visual drama. The *distance* of the worshiper from the liturgical action (not the closeness, so cherished in the buildings of Jones and Wren) helped shape a sense of transcendence, the other-ness of the holy. Ornate furnishings, in contrast to the simplicity of the seventeenth-century buildings, set the norm. The visual beauty of the building and its support for the dramatic aspects of the liturgy provided the rationale for what came to be called the neo-gothic style now familiar to every Episcopalian—the split choir across a lengthy chancel separating the people from the altar, pulpit on one side of the chancel, lectern on the other. The neo-gothic ambiance for worship contrasts sharply with the stately but oddly intimate assembly for the hearing of the word, an ideal from the earlier era. Neither the seventeenth-century rationalists nor the Cambridge Camden Society managed a Prayer Book revision. Their accomplishments in architecture, however, proved no less revolutionary in terms of their influence on worship.

Attention to the setting for worship likewise holds rich possibilities for us. Inattention to these matters, however, courts disaster. Attending to issues of architecture and setting will occasionally coincide with an opportunity for building a new church or under-taking major renovations in an existing structure. In that case, planners will do well to consider carefully *every* detail of the space for worship. Will that space fit the ideals for worship suggested in BCP 1979? Will it provide a visual balance for the Prayer Book's threefold emphasis on the dignity of the word, the sacrament of the table, and the sacrament of baptism? Will the space welcome a worshiping household of God, taking its beauty from the gathering of people? Or will it be more beautiful when it is empty? Will the space support the clear hearing of the word? And will its acoustics also invite people to sing heartily? Will the space suggest a sense of the people gathering as community—and not just let them show up as spectators? Asking hard (and subtle) questions like these can help planners dream their way into a new building.

Most of us, however, will have to learn to live creatively in the buildings we already have. Neither the neo-gothic (a most common sort) nor the rational style of architecture entirely supports the ideals of liturgical renewal evident in BCP 1979. Careful thought about the placement of the three liturgical centers (lectern, table, and font), in light of the questions above, suggests one example of how to make liturgical renewal a greater possibility in many of our older buildings. Lack of attention to these matters, however, can result in the sort of liturgical dissonance that is all too common: the renewed rites will find their way into a setting not at all in keeping with their meaning. The setting, in fact, can undermine any possibility for genuine renewal—especially if no one is thinking about the issues. BCP 1979 does not follow the neo-gothic template in architecture or ceremonial, with but a few changes in wording here and there. The renewal made possible in the Prayer Book is much more thorough-going than that.

The Love for Tradition—and Reasons to Suspect It

There is no doubt that Anglicanism draws deeply from the wells of Christian tradition. The reformers saw themselves as reconstructing ancient patterns of worship for the English people. This course formed one of their primary agendas. Richard Hooker gave Anglicanism a rich legacy of valuing tradition in his familiar threefold expression of authority: scripture, reason, and tradition. Seventeenth- and eighteenth-century appeals to Hooker usually listed the three elements in this order, one that may have an odd ring for contemporary Episcopalians. It is the order, however, implicit in Hooker's method. We have grown accustomed to the subtle reordering undertaken by the tractarians, who, treasuring the tradition dearly, shifted it to the middle term of these three to give prominence to their favored resource for authority.[43] Appeals to the tradition will do well to remember this earlier order, the more "traditional" rendering. Let us recognize, however, that quibbling over the correct way to render the threefold basis of authority can lead us astray, for Hooker emphasized the priority of scripture and the *dynamic* relationship among the three more than anything else. An unthinking traditionalism skews the appropriate expression of Anglicanism, but so does an untoward rationalism. Both tradition and reason (and yes, scripture also) can become idols. They exist not as ends in themselves but as servants of a living faith.

Problems abound when people make tradition unduly important or when they get confused about what constitutes tradition. Doing something the same way for three years in a row does not

---

[43]See, for example, Hooker, *Ecclesiastical Polity*, 3. 4. Paul Avis provides an excellent synthesis of Hooker's method in *Anglicanism and the Christian Church: Theological Resources in Historical Perspective* (Minneapolis: Fortress Press, 1989), 63–67.

necessarily graft that innovation onto the tradition of the church catholic. The innovation may very well meet the needs of a worshiping community, and it may be appropriate, a *reasonable* way to express its corporate praise of God. (The innovation may then find its entrance into the threefold dynamic of authority through reason, not tradition.) But doing something for three years, or forty years, or ninety-nine years does not in itself make that something traditional, in the strictest sense. Perhaps we can honor many such elements in the liturgy as conventions or customs while recognizing that they lack the dignity and authority of the tradition. Anglicanism looks to the tradition over the long haul, the centuries-long consensus that most often tells us about essentials, the broad strokes on the canvas. And for this consensus, Anglicanism looks especially to the resources of antiquity. The tradition often cannot inform us with all the details, but ironically it is the details that attract the most tenacious (and ill-informed) arguments about "tradition." The Anglican way, for example, does not stand or fall on which altar candle gets lighted first. Convention suggests such an order, but it is just that—a convention. Careful liturgical planners will learn not to brood over such details or to make more out of them than they deserve. Often the so-called "traditional reasons" for these actions actually obscure more than help. It is often said, for example, that the candle on the epistle side of the altar must be lighted before the candle on the gospel side, because "the gospel cannot stand without the epistle"— whatever that means. Does this suggest then that the epistle could stand without the gospel? And in most ceremonial these days, is it even helpful to distinguish between a gospel side and an epistle side? And yet it may be possible and desirable to follow a convention of lighting one candle before the other. Deliberate flouting of convention may serve no purpose. But the convention can be kept in perspective if the tradition is allowed to inform the *central actions* of eucharistic praying—taking, blessing, breaking, sharing. Indeed the tradition abounds with material to inform our eucharistic prayer. Controversies about lighting candles amounts to fussing around the edges.

The appeal to tradition will avail little if isolated occurrences in history become excuses for some new fad. "Someone in an English monastery in the twelfth century once did it this way" has little authority in terms of tradition. The question for tradition has to be: Does this new idea fit the broad consensus of the church throughout the ages? Or does the tradition in any way help us reach a new consensus different from but in continuity with the consensus going before? It cannot be, simplistically: Has anyone ever done it this way before? The latter approach easily gives way to liturgical eccentricity, and it also lacks resilience. The most ardent opponents of ordaining women often argue precisely on these grounds of "tradition." Since it has never been done (or so they argue), it cannot now be done. The more careful approach to the tradition, recognizing that the historical record has at best some ambiguous hints of women in orders during Christian antiquity, asks another question: Does the tradition, taken broadly, suggest or even mandate an *emerging* consensus on the ordination of women? The deep currents of the tradition, and not scattered antiquarian flotsam and jetsam, need to shape the life of a living faith and its worship.

Lex Orandi Lex Credendi

"The law of prayer is the law of belief."[44] And generally Anglicans do assent to this proposition—what we pray *is* what we believe.

---

[44] Prosper of Aquitaine (c. 390 – c. 463) provided the origins of this familiar saying with his words, *ut legem credendi lex statuat supplicandi*, "the law of praying establishes the law of believing."

The churches of the Anglican communion are not (in technical terms) "confessional." There is neither an Augsburg Confession (as with the Lutherans), nor a Westminster Confession (as with the Presbyterians) to guide the workings of Anglican theology. Anglicans also lack a seminal theologian, a Martin Luther or a John Calvin or a John Wesley. There is no foundational book of beliefs or a single important theologian in this tradition. Precise, classical arguments from doctrine have little success holding the attention of most Anglicans. Nor does doctrine express a cause for Anglican unity, as it does in the other churches of the reformation and even in the Roman Catholic Church. There is no confessional flag to wave, not even an overriding theological tenet like justification for Lutherans or predestination for the churches of Reformed Christianity.

But for Anglicans the consensus achieved through common prayer does provide a center point not only for practice but for belief. Thus the Book of Common Prayer bears scrutiny for all aspects of Anglican believing. And so BCP 1979 includes, for example, the order for the ordination of a bishop, despite the fact that this service will be used about once every decade or two in a given diocese. It is even then a matter for diocesan worship, not parochial worship. But this infrequently used service tells us what Anglicans believe about bishops in a way no other resource can. The way faithful people worship when gathering as the church to ordain a bishop tells Anglicans what they believe about bishops on all occasions. And so any practical concerns about omitting a little-used service from the book in order to save on printing costs has to give way to the principle of *lex orandi lex credendi*.

Yet the principle has its limitations—or rather its proper interpretation must take into account the issues of dynamics. Ways of believing emerge, while the ways of praying lag behind; thus the forms for praying at a given moment may not express adequately what the people actually believe. For example, a common seventeenth-century understanding about Christ's presence in the eucharist had much greater clarity than the Cranmerian language of the eucharistic prayer would allow.[45] Only with the Prayer Book reforms of this century have the eucharistic rites allowed options that express such a high understanding of Christ's presence, an understanding almost universal within ECUSA and rooted in the high-eucharistic teachings of the seventeenth century.

Furthermore, the theological inquiry of the past century has been phenomenal, drawing upon secular learning for insights and applications. The 1889 publication of a volume of essays edited by Charles Gore and entitled *Lux Mundi* marked one watershed in modern Anglican thinking.[46] The rounds of liturgical renewal resulting in BCP 1979 represent the first time ECUSA has really incorporated in prayer what have been widely accepted Anglican ideas about Christian believing since *Lux Mundi*. Thus, for example, all but one of the eucharistic prayers of BCP 1979—the historic prayer, Prayer 1 of Rite I—treat Christ's atonement not just in terms of his sacrificial death but also in terms of his life and resurrection. Here is a generously broad treatment of atonement like that expressed by Arthur Lyttelton in *Lux Mundi* and widely accepted for nearly a century.[47] It took ECUSA ninety years to

---

[45]See William R. Crockett, *Eucharist: Symbol of Transformation* (New York: Pueblo, 1989), 189–97, for an excellent discussion of the eucharistic teachings of Lancelot Andrewes, John Cosin, and Jeremy Taylor, along with several quotations from their writings. See also *Anglicanism: The Thought and Practice of the Church of England, Illustrated from the Religious Literature of the Seventeenth Century*, ed. Paul E. More and Frank L. Cross (London: SPCK, 1962), 467–97, for a compendium of quotations from seventeenth-century divines.

[46]Charles Gore, ed., *Lux Mundi: A Series of Studies in the Religion of the Incarnation* (London: John Murray, 1889).

[47]Arthur Lyttelton, "The Atonement," in ibid., 201–29.

express in prayer what most seminaries were teaching in theology —and what most clergy were preaching. In this case *lex orandi* has had to catch up with *lex credendi*, for earlier prayers (including Prayer 1 of Rite I) have equated atonement with sacrificial death. Herein lies a dynamic demanding our attention, especially as Anglicans continue to follow the principle of liturgical reform. We can expect that as images for God (including the feminine) emerge from the deeper tradition and as they grow in acceptance, these ways of believing will converge with an increasing gender-sensitivity in our language to shape new ways of praying. And as Anglicans pray in such a fashion, their lives will be more deeply converted to the ways of believing expressed in such prayers. *Lex orandi* is never static for people engaged in a living faith.[48]

Anglican Worship: Cool, Not Hot

The Anglican approach to liturgy depends more on repeated encounters with word and sacrament than on the effecting of emotional ardor. This is not to say that emotion lies beyond the pale of Anglicanism; Hooker, in fact, included emotion and experience within his broad category of reason, perhaps a more holistic expression of the human adventure than we compartmentalizing moderns find comfortable. But Anglicanism has not sought to manipulate the spiritual quest into an emotional response. Anglican worship does not have to conjure up certain kinds of feelings among the gathered people in order to celebrate its power and effect in human life. Liturgy does not massage the emotions to elicit a gauged response; liturgy helps a faithful community become aware of what God is doing among God's people

---

[48]See the volume entitled *Supplemental Liturgical Materials* for the most recent materials in this growing edge of liturgical praying in the Episcopal Church.

and in the life of the cosmos. The liturgy patiently waits. If the hearts of the people find no strange warming on a given Sunday, the liturgy is not then ineffectual or disappointing. Anglicans can trust the liturgy, word and sacrament, to convert the lives of the faithful. Anglican worship, accordingly, does not have to be subjected to the tyranny of melodrama or the relevance of the moment. The steady routine of word and sacrament charts out the means of grace. Urban T. Holmes III writes about some liturgical perils when we fail to give heed to this principle:

> The . . . danger is that we loose [sic] confidence in the liturgy to effect the deep transformation of our peoples' symbolic world. We push for an immediate payoff, a goosy feeling they can repent as soon as they walk out the church door. This leads to gimmickery or foolishness. I have heard it suggested that on the feast of the Ascension one might preach from a ladder leaning against the rood beam. More than one priest has ridden into his church on Palm Sunday on a donkey, which has provided much food for the local wits. There was a time in the 1960s when every church conference had to have helium-filled balloons at the closing eucharist.[49]

Anglicans have it in their legacy to find freedom from such antics. The challenge, however, comes in trusting the routine without lapsing into routinization. The riches of word and sacrament, celebrated and administered in a lackadaisical fashion, can land God's faithful people squarely in a rut. Anglican worship has an innate capacity for generating boredom.[50] Planners of worship need to understand the sense of liveliness so necessary to the liturgy without resorting to manipulation. Word and sacrament are living already, and planners do not have to make them alive or

---

[49]Urban T. Holmes III, *What Is Anglicanism?* (Wilton, CT: Morehouse-Barlow, 1982), 47.

[50]Elizabethan church-goers were notably unruly, given to any kind of irreverent antics to shake off the boredom that had set in, once the novelty of the rites had worn off. See Davies, *Theology and Worship*, 1:212–13.

even force them to do something specific for the gathering of the faithful. Planners do need to attend to the rhythms and movements intrinsic to the proclamation of the word and the celebration of the sacraments, so that the faithful might be brought more fully into these rhythms and movements. Here a light touch is appropriate, not a heavy hand, for Anglicans are free to trust living word and sacrament to have their way in our lives, in God's good time. We do not have to manipulate word and sacrament or "make" them relevant.

CHAPTER 2

The Daily Office

THE INTRODUCTORY SECTION ENTITLED "CONCERN-ing the Service of the Church" sets the tone for the rest of the 1979 Prayer Book, establishing the intent and purpose of the book and listing some basic rules. The first paragraph of this section reads:

> The Holy Eucharist, the principal act of Christian worship on the Lord's Day and other major Feasts, and Daily Morning and Evening Prayer, as set forth in this Book, are the regular services appointed for public worship in this Church.[1]

Sunday (and holy day) eucharist, daily offices[2]—these set the basic patterns for corporate prayer according to BCP 1979. This chapter considers some issues around the daily offices, services too often and mistakenly considered minor, even negligible, moments in the routine of worship.

---

[1] BCP 1979, 13.

[2] The term "office" (from the Latin *officium*, duty or performance of a task) is but a generic designation for the various rites of the church's daily prayer. So, for example, morning prayer might also be called "the morning office."

From the earliest times, Christians have gathered for daily prayer, typically in a pattern following the rhythms of the day.[3] Sunrise and sunset, those primary rhythms marked by the sun, have given believers two natural times for prayer every day—the praise of God for a new day and the praise of God for day's end. Noonday, bedtime, and midnight have also marked natural times of prayer for Christians, but not everywhere have these occasions given rise to prayer. That is, they have never claimed the universal appeal had by praying at sunrise and sunset. And where these lesser moments in the day's rhythm have been kept as times of prayer, the manner of praying has tended to be briefer and less intense than what we find at sunrise and sunset.

The foundations of Christian patterns of daily prayer in Jewish practices is well-documented.[4] Until the destruction of the Temple in the year 70 of the Common Era, the priests in Jerusalem offered daily sacrifices, morning and evening. Pious believers throughout the Jewish world, it appears, offered prayer at the hours of sacrifice, a practice typifying synagogue worship. These gatherings for psalmody, scripture, and corporate prayer had such a deep influence on Jewish piety that the practice of daily prayer survived the destruction of the Temple. Observant Jews still follow these ancient traditions, the same traditions that shaped the early Christian practice of gathering daily for corporate prayer.[5] God's faithful people called into the Christian covenant learned to pray daily—morning and evening, and the contours of this prayer were well-

---

[3]See, for example, *Hippolytus: A Text for Students*, trans. Geoffrey J. Cuming (Bramcote, England: Grove Booklets, 1976), sections 35, 41.

[4]Robert Taft, *The Liturgy of the Hours in East and West: The Origins of the Divine Office and Its Meaning for Today* (Collegeville, MN: The Liturgical Press, 1986), 3–11. See the scriptural roots for these patterns of prayer, particularly in the psalms—Psalm 57:17; 65:8; 88:13; 199:164 and 141:2.

[5]Luke 24:53; Acts 2:1,46; 4:23–31; 12:5,12.

established in the Jewish traditions with which the church claims continuity.

Daily prayer continued as a common practice for all or most of the Christian faithful until the fifth or sixth century. Prayer at morning and prayer at evening during this early period took a simple and straightforward shape from a limited repertoire of favorite psalms, brief readings from scripture, and the prayers (often in litany form). Ordinary Christian people found these occasions for worship accessible and familiar, and the offices seem to have had a widespread popularity. The rise of monasticism from the fifth century forward, however, began a centuries-long process that saw an increasingly complex routine for daily prayer. Ordinary Christian people would no longer find the daily offices, now shaped by monastic practices, either accessible or familiar. Daily prayer began to seem foreign, mysterious, and *extra*-ordinary, reserved for those Christians with a special calling. Gradually, daily prayer declined as an act of worship for all the faithful. From *all* or *most* of the faithful in the early church, the numbers involved in daily prayer declined to *most* or *some*, then finally to *some* or *just a few*—and those an especially pious few. In the later middle ages, the practice of daily prayer, shaped as it was by the complexities inherited from monasticism, became a duty specifically for the clergy. No longer a work of prayer for all the faithful people, the offices devolved into a clerical obligation.[6]

---

[6]Ordinary Christian people never completely lost a sense of these rhythms of prayer, and many layfolk never abandoned the routines. Even if they could not follow all the twists and turns and crazy rules in the breviaries (the technical name for the church's office-books), they could still follow the routine of prayer at the appropriate hours. Simplified "books of hours," based on the office prayers, took on a great popularity in the late middle ages, and they were widespread among the literate classes. Their popularity testifies to a lingering sense among the people that the rhythms of the day suggest a natural rhythm of prayer.

Thomas Cranmer's intent was to rework this extraordinarily complex tradition of daily prayer from the monastic tradition so all the faithful might join in. His reforms in the daily office, begun in 1543 and first established in BCP 1549, have grown into some of the most popular elements of Anglican worship. Anglicans have had a love affair with matins and evensong (morning prayer and evening prayer), for not only did Cranmer make the offices accessible to ordinary Christians, but he emphasized the celebratory notes from the monastic offices to give the Prayer Book offices a festive shape. Until BCP 1979, it could be argued that the daily offices offered a more celebratory temper than did the more penitential communion service. The "celebration" of the eucharist sometimes seemed a contradiction of terms! Cranmer's shaping of the offices remained a huge success in its own right, and he made it possible for Christian folk to praise God for the new day and to praise God for day's end. The extent of lay participation in the offices every day during Cranmer's time (and afterward) is not clear, and perhaps it has never been extensive.[7] Yet in the English church, praying the offices daily remains an obligation for the clergy, with the assumption that the offices will be said in the church.[8] Daily corporate prayer has thus always at least been available to ordinary Christians, and the rhythms and beauty of

---

[7] J. Wickham Legg, *English Church Life from the Restoration to the Tractarian Movement* (London: Longmans, Green and Co., 1914), 94–110.

[8] As noted in Chapter One, BCP 1552 sets contradictory norms for the clergy's obligation to pray the office. The rubrics state that the office *will* take place in the church—but the section "Concerning the Service of the Church" allows the cleric to pray the office either in public *or in private*! BCP 1662 follows this contradictory path, also. See Brightman, *English Rite*, 1:38–39, 127. The American Prayer Books have not mandated the office as a daily obligation for the clergy. Even so, the first American revision, BCP 1789, stressed the every-day expectations for the offices by adding "Daily" to the title of both morning prayer and evening prayer. Marshall, *Prayer Book Parallels*, 1:86–87.

the offices have arguably affected the piety of ordinary Anglicans as much as any other aspect of the Prayer Book.

The Office as the Norm for Daily Prayer

As BCP 1979 clearly states, the offices give the form and structure to daily worship, while the eucharist gives the form and structure to worship on Sundays and other holy days. The historic Prayer Books as well as BCP 1979 offer a lectionary for Morning and Evening Prayer. They do not include a lectionary for daily eucharist, a significant point to consider for planning daily worship.[9] The rounds of every-day prayer typifying Anglicanism take their shape in these liturgies of the word praising God for the new day and for day's end.[10] Daily "mass," although grafted into the customary practice of many Anglicans through the catholic revival in the nineteenth century, remains a curiosity, even an anomaly, in the Prayer Book way.

A parish that displaces the Sunday celebration of the eucharist with morning prayer misunderstands the opening paragraph in "Concerning the Service of the Church" quoted above. That parish not only misses the genius of BCP 1979, but more important it also fails to recognize the fundamental linkage between Lord's Day (day of resurrection, day of creation, day of the Spirit's coming,

---

[9]Note, however, that *Lesser Feasts and Fasts*, 19–41, includes optional eucharistic propers for "The Weekdays of Advent and Christmas until the Baptism of Christ," "The Weekdays of Lent," and "The Weekdays of Easter Season." The point remains that this volume lacks the normative force of the Prayer Book.

[10]The office's use of the Apostles' Creed, associated with baptism from antiquity, brings a *daily* recollection of baptism to the worshipers. See Hamon L'Estrange, *The Alliance of Divine Offices*, 4th ed. (Oxford: John Henry Parker, 1846; 1st ed., 1690), 116–20. Also, the power of the invitatory Psalm 95, the Venite, lies in v. 7: "Oh, that *today* you would hearken to his voice!" See Wheatly, *Rational Illustration*, 3. 8.

etc.) and eucharist. Lord's Day and eucharist belong together, and it is fair to say that the Episcopal Church has reached a broad consensus on this point. Most parishes celebrate the eucharist as their chief act of worship every Sunday, and probably most Episcopalians appreciate the rationale behind such a practice.

The corollary norm, that morning prayer and evening prayer give shape to everyday prayer in Prayer Book practice, lacks such a clear consensus, at least as reflected in the parishes of ECUSA. Let us begin with an admission that life's rhythms in the contemporary American setting usually make it difficult for people to gather for daily prayer. Our routines, removed from the rural and village life in which Cranmer's reforms mostly first took root, often put us out of synch with the rhythms of the day and make it impossible for a scattered community of people to gather daily. A priest ministering in a busy and scattered community may also find scheduling the offices and being present for them problematic. But even in these difficult circumstances, a parish still can decide to maintain a routine of daily corporate prayer. Is attendance likely to be spotty? Let us remember that daily prayer in actual practice in Anglicanism has seldom found large numbers present. Can the priest not always be there? The Prayer Book allows lay people to officiate at the offices, and says as much in "Concerning the Service of the Church" as well as in the rubrics for the offices.[11] A commitment *by the community* and not just by the priest can encourage a discipline of daily corporate prayer. The Prayer Book, moreover, provides planners with a wide-ranging flexibility for shaping the offices, as careful reading of the rubrics will show. There are many choices to be made, and the offices can take an uncomplicated shape, one that need not be burdensome at all. The lectionary in BCP 1979 even tacitly recognizes that a

---

[11]BCP 1979, 13, 36, 74.

parish may choose to pray the office but once daily, for the section from "Concerning the Daily Office Lectionary" reads:

> Three Readings are provided for each Sunday and weekday in each of the two years. Two of the Readings may be used in the morning and one in the evening; or, *if the Office is read only once in the day,* all three Readings may be used.[12]

The flexibility extends this far.

A parish that establishes a corporate norm for praying the office can provide a point of reference for those who will pray the office as a devotion, a part of the routine of their private prayer. A person who can pray with the community even occasionally can enrich his or her solitary praying of the office—and understand that such a solitary practice, necessary as it may be, is not the norm. The office as devotion is derivative, but it can be a legitimate practice nonetheless, even if it is less than ideal. The person with a praying community as a point of reference can follow its customs and manners about using the office, avoiding unduly idiosyncratic and eccentric practices in the process. The solitary person praying the office then can be drawn more fully into his or her use of the church's daily worship, recognizing a concrete (not abstract) communal basis for what he or she does.

The Prayer Book norm about offices and daily prayer may deserve to be brought to bear on a troubling aspect of Episcopal Church life. Liturgical renewal has brought to the Episcopal Church, thankfully, a renewed appreciation for the eucharist, but sometimes this appreciation breaks loose from any association with Lord's Day and holy day. It often seems that every gathering of Episcopalians demands a eucharist. Vestry meetings begin or end with eucharist. Other parish organizations follow suit. Clergy meet weekly for breakfast or lunch—and eucharist. No diocesan

---

[12]BCP 1979, 934. Emphasis added.

meeting, large or small, is complete without it. Workshops and conferences of every kind often assume that eucharist will find a place in the schedule. The Episcopal Church is heavily eucharistic. Is it overly eucharistic? The recovery of eucharist in the life of the church is commendable, but having a eucharist apart from considering the calendar (Is it Sunday? Is it a holy day?) can cause us to lose something precious from our heritage, the sensibility of the office as ordinary daily prayer and the rhythms of the week. It is possible, according to our heritage, for a gathered community to celebrate Christ's presence through the hearing of word and offering of prayer. Christ's presence can be known through means other than the bread and wine of the eucharist. Sometimes celebrating his presence in the gathering of community and the hearing of word is the more appropriate approach, according to Prayer Book practice and ancient tradition. The ancients, after all, always celebrated eucharist on the Lord's Day—but only then. The liturgy of the word formed daily prayer, and these early believers never imagined that anything was "missing" from such a practice. In the office prayer dating from BCP 1662, we still can pray the ancient Prayer of St. Chrysostom, and trust that when two or three are gathered in Jesus' name, God will be in our midst.[13]

The Psalter as Infrastructure of the Office and Basic Song of the Church

The monastic office draws heavily on the psalter for its content. Anyone who has prayed with a monastic or religious community understands that a monk or nun would have to develop a deep love for the psalms, for any community inspired by the rule of

---

[13]BCP 1979, 59, 72, 102, 126. Cf. Brightman, *English Rite*, 1:151. The Prayer of St. Chrysostom derives from Matthew 18:20.

Benedict might spend hours every day praying its way through them. Monastics who strictly follow this rule make their way through the whole psalter every week. However adapted, a generous and daily use of the psalter undergirds the whole of monastic prayer and piety.[14]

When Cranmer restructured and simplified the office for pastoral use in the parishes, he retained the psalm-rich structure for the office, adapting its spirituality to the needs of ordinary churchgoers. Cranmer's adaptation for the first Prayer Books 1549 and 1552 set forth a thirty-day cycle of psalms rather than a seven-day monastic cycle—but in two offices per day, instead of the monastic seven. The Anglican office, from Cranmer forward, has depended on the psalter for its basic content and as a foundation for prayer. Hooker argued that the psalter's central place in the office is reasonable, since more than any other scripture, the psalms orient the worshiper toward God. The psalms teach the worshiper to pray; and more than that, the psalms are prayer.[15]

Hooker also argued for the singing of psalms as a means of bringing the worshiper more fully into this scriptural prayer.[16] The psalter, from earliest times, has provided the basic core of the church's song, and Anglicans have experimented with diverse schemes for singing the psalms, especially since this basic song undergirds the church's daily prayer. In the years following BCP 1549, both plainchant and harmonized chant found favor in English churches, and for nearly a hundred years this tradition flourished. But the English Civil War in the 1640s saw the demise

---

[14]*St. Benedict's Rule for Monasteries*, trans. Leonard J. Doyle, sections 9–20 (Collegeville, MN: The Liturgical Press, 1948), 30–41. Cf. Taft, *Liturgy of the Hours*, 122–40.

[15]Hooker, *Ecclesiastical Polity*, 5. 37. 2.

[16]Ibid., 5. 38.

of chant as popular song, with metrical psalmody taking its place. Already prevalent in puritan circles, this form translated (or rather, paraphrased) the psalms into verse, often a rhyming verse, and set the words to familiar tunes. Metrical psalmody became commonplace everywhere in English churches.[17] Perhaps the most familiar metrical psalm tune in the English-speaking world is *Old 100th* (*The Hymnal 1982*, 377 and 378), the tune many will know as "The Doxology." This text in the hymnal is actually a metrical version of Psalm 100. Compare the Prayer Book text of the first verse of the psalm,

> Be joyful in the Lord, all you lands;*
>   serve the Lord with gladness
>   and come before his presence with a song[18]

with this metrical paraphrase,

> All people that on earth do dwell,
>   sing to the Lord with cheerful voice:
> him serve with mirth, his praise forth tell,
>   come ye before him and rejoice.[19]

Other such tunes include the likes of *Dundee* (*The Hymnal 1982*, 126, 526, 709) and *Caithness* (*The Hymnal 1982*, 121, 352, 684).

Thus we have the two prevalent strands for singing the psalms in Anglican practice. Chant, revived in the aftermath of the Oxford movement, has the advantage of a greater flexibility than the metrical tunes because planners can find chants ranging from the

---

[17] A study of the development of these two strains of song is both complex and compelling. See the pertinent essays in *The Hymnal 1982 Companion*, 2 vols., ed. Raymond F. Glover (New York: Church Hymnal Corporation, 1990), especially Robin Leaver, "Plainchant Adaptation in England," 160–93, and "English Metrical Psalmody," 321–48; Ruth M. Wilson, "Harmonized Chant," 215–37; and Charles G. Manns, "Psalmody in America to the Civil War," 393–416.

[18] BCP 1979, 729.

[19] *The Hymnal 1982*, 377, 378.

very simple to the most intricate and musically interesting. The simpler style of chant might suit the musical needs of congregational singing; the intricate style could draw on the resources of a choir. Chant also has the advantage of matching the music to the text, not the other way around, as in metrical psalmody. On the other hand, metrical psalmody is eminently singable, with or without accompaniment. And good rhythmic translations of the psalms can bring new insights; they do not have to obscure the meaning or result in doggerel. But a major disadvantage in metrical psalmody lies in its dullness, a factor that becomes too apparent after twenty verses or so of uninspired paraphrase set to a monotonous tune. The eighteenth-century priest John Brown writes:

> But while we justly admire the *sacred Poetry* of our *Cathedral* Service, must we not lament the State of it in our *parochial* Churches, where the cold, the meagre, the disgusting *Dulness* of STERNHOLD and his *Companions*, hath *quenched* all the *poetic Fire* and *devout Majesty* of the *royal Psalmist*.[20]

Yet despite the differences in the two major styles, the point of singing the psalms as an Anglican preference becomes clear from the tradition. The ancient Hebrew book of songs became the first Christian hymnal, a source for singing traditionally cherished by Anglicans—at times to the exclusion of singing anything else (including hymns). Planners can take this traditional *preference* seriously in considering the shape of the office in their locale, weighing that possibility against the value of saying the psalms. Chant, accessible and flexible, seems to have won the day, and various resources for psalm chant are available.[21] But metrical

---

[20]John Brown, quoted in Legg, *English Church Life*, 187. Emphasis in the original. Thomas Sternhold (d. 1549) was one of the first and most prolific versifiers of metrical psalmody.

[21]The most important include *The Anglican Chant Psalter*, ed. Alec Wyton (New York: Church Hymnal Corporation, 1987); *The Plainsong Psalter*, ed. James

psalmody is not out of place, and some may opt for that strain of the tradition.[22]

Reading the psalms will nonetheless remain an obvious choice for many parishes, especially when a congregation is likely to be small, but even here the options are many. The section, "Concerning the Psalter," in BCP 1979 begins:

> The Psalter is a body of liturgical poetry. It is designed for vocal, congregational use, whether by singing or reading. There are several traditional methods of psalmody. The exclusive use of a single method makes the recitation of the Psalter needlessly monotonous.[23]

The Prayer Book then details four methods of recitation, whether by reading or singing: direct recitation (unison); antiphonal recitation (alternating verses by different sections of the worshiping community); responsorial recitation (a single, repeating refrain for the congregation, while the choir or cantor or reader sings or says the verses of the psalm); and responsive recitation (a minister alternating verses with the congregation.)[24] With whatever method, reading the psalms should be natural, prayerful, unforced, and without affectation. The asterisk in the psalm, an important marker in the poetry, unfortunately attracts affectation, especially that unnaturally long pause between half-verses (a common practice in some monastic communities, the source of this increasingly popular way of saying the psalms). The Prayer

---

Litton (New York: Church Hymnal Corporation, 1988); and *The Hymnal 1982, Accompaniment Edition*, 2 vols. (New York: Church Hymnal Corporation, 1985), 1:S408–15, for Simplified Anglican Chants.

[22]See the list of *The Hymnal 1982*'s metrical psalms in *The Hymnal 1982 Accompaniment*, 1:679. A comprehensive metrical psalter comes in the hymnal of the Christian Reformed Church, *The Psalter Hymnal* (Grand Rapids, MI: Eerdmans, 1987).

[23]BCP 1979, 582.

[24]Ibid.

Book notes a *distinct* pause at the asterisk, and it should signal a clear break without leaving the worshipers guessing when to begin again with the second half-verse. Affectations like this, with good intentions for fostering a meditative sensibility, usually detract from the natural cadences of the words in this ancient poetry-become-prayer.

The lectionary in BCP 1979 takes a tack more sensitive to the time of day and to the church season than did earlier lectionaries built around a thirty-day cycle, which took the psalms in course. With the current lectionary, the Prayer Book no longer appoints psalms associated with evening for morning prayer, for example. No longer is Psalm 114 (formerly appointed for evening prayer on the twenty-third of the month), a Passover psalm associated with Easter in Christian practice, likely to show up in Holy Week but not in Easter Week! BCP 1979 uses italics to note the old thirty-day psalm lectionary throughout the psalter itself, thus preserving this convention from earlier Prayer Books.[25] But its presence should not suggest to planners that it is a likely alternative to the more carefully considered seven-week psalm cycle in the office lectionary.

The Offices and Scripture

One of Cranmer's intents in reforming the office lay in his desire to instruct English churchpeople in the scriptures. This didactic principle gave the office one of its distinctive strengths as well as a weakness. The course reading of the Bible, one chapter after another, one reading from the Old Testament and one from the

---

[25]It should be noted BCP 1789 started a movement away from this convention, at least allowing options to the psalms appointed in the thirty-day cycle. This movement continued through BCP 1892 and BCP 1928. A substantial lectionary revision in 1943 anticipated the psalm cycle found in BCP 1979.

New Testament at each office, put daily worshipers in contact—repetitive contact—with the scriptures. The same book from the Old Testament would be read for the first lesson at both offices, one chapter at morning prayer, the next chapter at evening prayer, continuing with this pattern as long as necessary to complete the book. Morning Prayer's second lesson applied this method of course reading though the gospels and the book of Acts; evening prayer's second lesson came from the New Testament epistles. The course reading was but rarely interrupted, and then only for the most major of holy days. And thus the reformers found a way of informing and strengthening a biblical faith for the English church.[26] The first Prayer Book was especially sensitive to the power of course readings in shaping the faith of Christian people:

> [T]he people (by daily hearyng of holy scripture read in the Churche) should continuallye profite more and more in the knowlege of God, and bee the more inflamed with the loue of his true religion-.
>
> -But these many yeares passed, this Godly and decent ordre of the auncient fathers, hath bee so altered, broken, and neglected, by planting in vncertain stories, Legēdes, Respondes, Verses, vaine repiticions, Commemoracions and Synodalles, that commonly when any boke of the Bible was begon: before three or four Chapiters were read out, all the rest were vnread. And in this sorte, the boke of Esaie was begon in Aduent, and the booke of Genesis in Septuagesima: but they were onely begon, and neuer read thorow. After a like sorte wer other bokes of holy scripture vsed.[27]

Often, however, people found themselves overwhelmed if not bored by all this scripture. But if this much Bible was simply too much for most people to take in, its use in the office nonetheless has had an undeniable effect on the spirituality of Anglicans for more than four hundred years.[28] The Prayer Book offices have

---

[26]See the daily lectionaries in Brightman, *English Rite*, 1:46–124.

[27]Brightman, *English Rite*, 1:34.

[28]See Martin Thornton, *English Spirituality: An Outline of Ascetical Theology According to the English Pastoral Tradition* (London: SPCK, 1963), 271, 277.

given to anyone bending to this discipline an undying familiarity with the Bible. Often this occurs at a conscious, cognitive level, but at other times it forms the believer in ways that are unconscious and even precognitive. William Temple's experience with the offices during his childhood testifies to the effect of this routinized, daily exposure to scripture through the offices. Growing up a bishop's son, Temple, from his earliest recollections, found himself in the chapel every day for the offices, and this routine left an undeniable impression on him, as he wrote some fifty years later to a friend who had had a similar childhood experience:

> I am constantly thinking of the enormous difference that it must have made to you and me that from a date before we could clearly remember things, we heard some verses of the Bible read every day; probably three times out of five we did not directly attend to it; but it was flowing over our growing minds, even when attention wandered, and must have been producing a great effect in making natural and spontaneous that whole outlook upon life which the Bible expresses.[29]

These large chunks of scripture, read daily according to the Prayer Book discipline, have had their effect in familiarizing Anglicans with the Bible, albeit in an uncritical fashion. But Anglicans have trusted the Bible—even to the point of not insisting on a sermon at the offices to interpret the scriptures for the people. In fact, as noted in Chapter One, the reformers provided no place for a sermon in the Prayer Book offices, much to the chagrin of the puritans, who emphasized the place of preaching as an act of worship.

But so much Bible, set forth trustingly and without interpreta-

---

[29]William Temple, in F. A. Iremonger, *William Temple, Archbishop of Canterbury: His Life and Letters* (London: Oxford University Press, 1948), 5. Temple's father, Frederick Temple, Bishop of Exeter during the years to which this letter refers, was later to become Archbishop of Canterbury 1897–1902). William Temple was Archbishop during the years 1942–44.

tion, with all its merits, nonetheless points toward an often unrecognized weakness in the Anglican offices. Morning prayer and evening prayer arose in the Christian tradition as occasions for praising God for the new day and for day's end. Such a heavily didactic purpose as we find in the historic Prayer Book offices can obscure this basic tenet of praise. The offices are not primarily about teaching, as valuable as that can be; they are primarily about praising God, in rhythm with the day. The reformers set out to make the offices a rich occasion for hearing the word. They perhaps did not realize that this wordladen shape of prayer could detract from other basic (and ancient) attitudes toward daily worship.

BCP 1979 follows the basic Anglican sensibility toward scripture in the offices, establishing course readings as the norm. The offices remain rich in use of scripture. This Prayer Book, however, has chosen a two-year lectionary as a base, making it possible to have readings shorter by half, just on that basis. BCP 1979, editing the course readings for both sense and suitability, also takes a more critical stance toward scripture than did earlier Prayer Books, paring down the amount of scripture even more. Thus not every chapter of every book gets read. Furthermore, BCP 1979 allows flexibility in choosing the readings. An office, morning or evening, can use one, two, or three readings. Readings may be lengthened at the discretion of worship planners. The instructions for the lectionary allow planners to lengthen, combine, or omit sections of scripture when a major feast interrupts the readings in course. For special occasions, the instructions also provide for the choice of psalms and readings besides those in the lectionary.[30]

This Prayer Book thus sets forward a daily office lectionary, still with ample portions of scripture but with a flexibility heretofore

---

[30]BCP 1979, 934–35.

unknown. Planners, accordingly, need to consider carefully the options before them and the needs of their worshiping community. Two points of reference can help in the planning. First, BCP 1979 honors the traditional Anglican value placed on sizable portions of scripture read in daily worship, and choices can be made without violating that deep-seated value. But a second point of reference is equally important, for this Prayer Book allows planners to recover daily prayer more authentically as occasions for praise of God, so the offices need not become mere excuses for the piling on of scripture. Careful planners will seek a balance between these two points of reference—scripture and praise.

The Responses to Scripture: Canticles, Sermons, Silence

The psalter is not the only source of biblical song, for poetry is intrinsic to the biblical method of God's revealing self to humankind. Often the story of God's revelation takes shape in song, and just as often the human response finds the same shape. Some of these songs from scripture have made their way into worship, from the church's earliest days—such songs as the Song of Mary and the Song of Simeon, in Luke's gospel.[31] Other scriptural songs have provided direct inspiration for ancient songs of the church, *Gloria in Excelsis* and *Te Deum* the two most familiar examples to Episcopalians. These two are not songs directly from the Bible, but they are so closely akin to the scriptural songs that they belong in the same category called *canticles*. BCP 1979 has drawn its canticles from a rich tradition, giving us a wider repertoire of scriptural (and scripture-based) song than in any previous Prayer Book—twenty-one canticles in all.[32] These canticles provide the

---

[31]Luke 1:46–55; 2:39–32.

[32]Or fourteen, taking into account the seven canticles in both traditional and

worshipers an opportunity to respond in praise to the proclaimed word, and they help bridge the first reading to the second, the second reading to the creed.[33]

The multiplicity of options again requires worship planners to make choices. The Prayer Book prints a table of suggestions for the office canticles. And although the table offers an excellent and carefully planned rotation for the canticles, its offerings remain suggestions.[34] Rigidity and assumptions based on the practice mandated by earlier Prayer Books need especially to be avoided: "Morning prayer must always include The Song of Zechariah." "The *Gloria in Excelsis* belongs in the eucharist and has no place in morning prayer." "The evening office has to have the Song of Mary and the Song of Simeon, and no other canticles will do." The current Prayer Book offers many more choices than its predecessors, and the earlier, more restrictive rules do not apply. BCP 1979 has raided the treasury from ancient sources and has recovered office canticles used in various locales, from Spain to Asia Minor and Egypt, to enrich the canticle repertoire. The Prayer Book also sets aside assumptions about certain canticles, such as the *Gloria in Excelsis*, and makes it possible for worshipers to recover the richness of their use in the early church. The *Gloria*, after all, had its beginning as an office hymn (not as a part of the mass) and is still used as such in the Eastern churches.[35] Communities who pray the offices daily will want to develop some plan for using

---

contemporary language. No earlier Prayer Book had more than six, although some Prayer Books (1552 and following) printed psalms as alternatives to some of the canticles.

[33]L'Estrange, *Alliance of Divine Offices*, 115; and Wheatly, *Rational Illustration*, 3. 13.

[34]BCP 1979, 144–45.

[35]Marion J. Hatchett, *Commentary on the American Prayer Book* (New York: Seabury, 1981), 117.

all the richness available in the various canticles. Special occasions and attention to the lectionary may suggest certain choices deviating from the usual cycle, but a general scheme like that suggested in the Prayer Book (and described above) can help establish a norm for using the canticles—all and not just some—and to use them suitably, with meaning for the feast or season or day of the week.[36]

BCP 1979 is the first Prayer Book to provide in its rubrics the option for another sort of response to the scriptures, that of corporate silence. The silence following the spoken word can punctuate the liturgy and provide the worshipers with an opportunity to reflect on the reading. This liturgical silence also inculcates a sense of reverence and community. Sometimes the most legitimate response to the proclaimed word is to say nothing, to do nothing, but sit silently with fellow believers. Purposeful, corporate silence like this nurtures a sense of community, and usually does so on an unconscious level, one that is to be trusted.

This sensibility raises the question: Should there be a sermon? The rubrics allow the option of a sermon "after the Office; or, within the Office, after the Readings or at the time of the hymn or anthem after the Collects."[37] Planners should weigh two factors. The first is the traditional Anglican willingness to let the scriptures speak for themselves. Sermons are necessary but not necessary on every occasion, and in fact sometimes they are out of place.[38] The second is a pastoral desire and responsibility to break open the word, especially evident when the course reading through the

---

[36]See ibid., 112–21, for the historic associations between the various canticles and the calendar. Some canticles have associations with particular days of the week; others evidence a strong connection with one or more of the seasons or festivals.

[37]BCP 1979, 142.

[38]Hooker, *Ecclesiastical Polity*, 5. 21.

office lectionary takes the worshipers through an odd or confusing stretch of scripture.

Lengthy sermons clearly destroy the balance and flow of the office. The old-style Sunday sermon at morning prayer, lasting upwards of thirty minutes, disrupts the movement of the office. On the other hand, a carefully crafted homily, lasting a few minutes, could fit within the structure of the office without overwhelming everything else. Planners could judiciously include such a sermon in the office. They could also legitimately exclude a sermon, understanding with Hooker that the scriptures bring a power in themselves, and that the offices might be one occasion for attending to that power.

The Prayers as Summation and Conclusion

The office's work of praying does not begin with the section called "The Prayers." The prayers articulate and bring to conclusion some aspects of the praying that have gone before—in the psalms, in the prayerful attention to the scriptures, in the silences, and in the scriptural song. To arrange the liturgies of daily prayer in such a fashion to suggest that "The Prayers" are radically set apart from the rest of office is to misunderstand the office's structure.

At the head of this section comes the Lord's Prayer, followed by two options for suffrages. Then come the collects, notable for their terseness, their "comprehensive brevity,"[39] and their form, "as rigid in structure as a sonnet or haiku."[40] This precision in form provides for concision in statement, and the collect sums up (that is, it literally *collects*) various aspects of prayer implicit from the occasion, the season, or the particular intercessory needs of the

---

[39]Wheatly, *Rational Illustration*, 3. 19. 2.

[40]Hatchett, *Commentary on the American Prayer Book*, 164.

worshipers.[41] An officiant can undermine the artful and prayerful concision of the collects by reading prayer after prayer after prayer —the collect for the day, all the collects in the office proper,[42] additional collects from elsewhere in the Prayer Book, the General Thanksgiving, and the Prayer of St. Chrysostom. The officiant can choose among the prayers, with the understanding that less can be more, and that summations are often content to leave something unsaid.

Ambiance of the Rite and Ceremonial: Plain or Fancy?

Worship planners may lament whenever their parish lacks the resources for exuberant celebrations of the offices, like the even-song of English cathedrals—vested choir (perhaps a boy-choir), grand music befitting a building that is grander still, processions and incense and clergy in copes and all the rest. Episcopalians are prone to pine after this model for the office and sometimes assume that it is the norm from which all celebrations of the office must derive.[43] (Actually, this attitude toward cathedral-style evensong often makes up in romanticism what it lacks in authenticity.) BCP 1979 offers no such assumption for the ambiance of the daily office. And although morning prayer and evening prayer can be adapted to the style of offices in some of the English cathedrals, close examination of the rites reveals other, more likely tacks to

---

[41]See Wheatly, *Rational Illustration*, 3. 19.

[42]Notice that there are seven collects in this section, including three specifically designated for Sundays, Fridays, and Saturdays. An officiant might reasonably choose one of the remaining collects to use in turn on the other four days of the week. See Hatchett, *Commentary on the American Prayer Book*, 125.

[43]See John David Chambers, *Divine Worship in England in the Thirteenth and Fourteenth Centuries Contrasted with and Adapted to that in the Nineteenth*, rev. ed. (London: Basil Montagu Pickering, 1877), 99–127, for a model of evensong in the ritualist tradition.

take. The offices in BCP 1979 suggest less the ideal of choral performance than a community gathering to pray, with music as the servant of the gathering, not its primary purpose. BCP 1979 does not even allow the office to begin with a hymn or anthem! Perhaps a single, well-chosen office hymn (after the collects) will provide a better balance to the office than will the piling up of hymnody and anthems. The general shape of the offices suggests a muted and reflective style, participatory, regular and familiar. That elaborate model for sung choral offices might detract from the divine monotony, the routine so essential to a corporate spirituality of the offices. It is a monotony not in the sense of boredom but the sense of familiarity, regularity, bringing the worshipers into the divine rhythm and the rhythms of the day—the new day and day's end. The ceremonial style to support this approach to worship would be low-key and without excess, a style any community of worshipers would have the resources to support. Pining away after what we think goes on in English cathedrals may divert our attention from important possibilities with the resources at hand.

Even so, the Prayer Book offices retain the flexibility to support a choral celebration, with a choir singing all the psalms, all the canticles, and an anthem. But the people's parts are clearly marked in the rite, and these may not be sung by the choir alone.[44] Interestingly, the service called "An Order of Worship for the Evening" (BCP, 108–14), an innovation in Anglican practice, invites a more elaborate ceremonial style than does morning prayer or evening prayer. The order for evening derives from forms for daily prayer from the early church as it developed in the parishes—not in the monasteries.[45] Although flexible enough to adapt for use as a

---

[44]The opening versicle and *Gloria Patri*, the Apostles' Creed, and the Lord's Prayer are to be sung or said by all.

[45]The technical term for this style of service is "cathedral office," to distinguish it from the monastic office. Despite the terminology, the cathedral office is not to be

longer meal prayer in a home, this Prayer Book service finds its most festive expression in a fuller ceremonial style. The drama of lighting candles in darkness (and the haunting music to accompany this action[46]), an optional provision for incense, the mention of all four orders of ministry in the section "Concerning the Service," the solemnity of the prayers—all these factors imply a rich but carefully considered ceremonial. For an office with the ceremonial richness that nourishes the spiritual life of many Episcopalians, here is the resource.

Noonday and Compline: Minor Notes in the Day's Rhythm

In adapting the offices for his purposes, Cranmer chose to focus entirely on prayers for the new day and for day's end, providing no rites for other moments in the rhythm of the day—noonday, bedtime, or midnight. Cranmer's course was to simplify what had become an inordinately complex round of monastic prayer, and accordingly he eliminated all the offices but two. Among his simplifications, he incorporated some materials from compline (prayers at bedtime) into evensong, and he eliminated the three "little offices" in the middle of the day (terce, sext, and none— 9 A.M., 12 noon, and 3 P.M., respectively).[47]

BCP 1979 recovers two of these offices as options—"An Order of Service for Noonday" (BCP, 103–7) and "An Order for Compline" (127–35). Not assumed as part of the church's normative routine of prayer (daily morning and evening prayer and Sunday eucharist are that), these offices nonetheless provide a worshiping community with the resources for punctuating the day with praise

---

confused with the style of offices in the English cathedrals, discussed above.

[46]*The Hymnal 1982: Service Music Accompaniment Edition,* Volume 1, S305–20.

[47]Hatchett, *Commentary on the American Prayer Book,* 92–93, 132, 144.

of God. They may prove helpful in this regard, even if they do not form a part of the community's prayer every day. A group meeting from 11 A.M. to 2 P.M., for example, would find the two major offices out of synch with their gathering.[48] Prayers about the new day or the day's end are jarring when they are offered when the sun is at its highest! The noonday office in BCP 1979 addresses this need. The office can be said in brief fashion, as printed in the Prayer Book, or it can be expanded with alternative readings and psalmody, if a richer liturgy of the word is desired. Compline can be used in the same fashion late in the evening or at bedtime. These two offices help planners maintain a sensitivity to the day's rhythms and the work of God through these rhythms—a basic sensibility giving life to the offices in the first place.

---

[48] The noonday office contains collects, lessons, and psalms appropriate to 9 A.M., noon, and 3 P.M., offering the possibility of a full monastic cycle of "little offices," if planners so choose. For example, the section of Psalm 119, the Romans 5:5 reading and the first of the collects could provide prayers for mid-morning. Psalm 121, the 2 Corinthians reading, and either the second or third collect could be used at noon. Psalm 126, the Malachi reading, and the last of the four collects could then be used at mid-afternoon.

CHAPTER 3

Baptism and Confirmation

THE FIRST WAVE OF LITURGICAL RENEWAL IN THIS century brought the eucharist to the center of parish life and made it the norm for the chief act of worship every Sunday. This recovery of the eucharist, widely lauded as a major accomplishment of liturgical renewal to date, had first to overcome the resistance of many Episcopalians. Despite a popular tendency to suppose this resistance lay in Episcopalians' unwillingness to take the eucharist seriously, in fact it was a profound, often undervalued attitude of reverence for the sacrament that underlay the struggle.

The piety common to Episcopalians not so long ago (and an honorable piety it was) steeped faithful churchpeople in an appreciation for the word, celebrated primarily in weekly morning prayer, with a concurrent and deeply abiding respect for the communion service. The prevalent strain of the Anglican heritage in ECUSA (Scottish, non-juring, and high church) has never treated the eucharistic celebration lightly, even when the celebrations have been few and far between. This high regard for the eucharist meant, for example, that communicants learned to prepare carefully before receiving the sacrament, and they learned the importance of knowing the sacrament's meaning. Infrequent communion, the most common eucharistic practice in former days, only heightened the sense of awe surrounding the sacrament. Even many anglo-catholic parishes with weekly celebrations did not necessarily encourage frequent communion from church-people. A "non-communicating mass" became a common Sunday liturgy in the most serious-minded anglo-catholic parishes. Perceptive clergy recognized that Episcopalians had a profound eucharistic piety, even when weekly communion had never been a part of their experience. And those leaders working toward a weekly celebration of the eucharist discovered in this piety a resource upon which to build. Even so, in the Episcopal Church the movement from weekly morning prayer to weekly eucharist took place over years and decades, not weeks and months. The naming of a popular spirituality, honoring it, and redirecting its energies required patience. Those who made their way through this recovery of the eucharist as the chief act of worship on Sunday did so by their honesty (that is, by refusing to pretend that "this is really the same as before and you will never notice the difference"), through their willingness to respect the people's sense of loss (and to give them space to grieve it), and through a long-sighted vision with its requisite patience.

A second wave of the liturgical movement is now taking the church toward a renewal of baptismal practices and understandings. This second wave, however, presents even more challenges to pastor and people than did the first, for BCP 1979 forces a complete rethinking of baptism and confirmation. The current Prayer Book clearly gives Episcopalians a logical progression from the earlier Prayer Book tradition of baptism. But proponents of a renewed sense of baptism need a discipline of honesty more than ever. A priest who says that "this is really the same as before and you will never notice the difference" when arguing for the renewed rites of baptism dissembles too much—or else fails to understand the issues. BCP 1979 looks through the Anglican tradition into the legacies from the early church and the Bible, highlighting those expressions of Anglicanism that put us in touch with these deeper, more ancient sensibilities. The result gives the Episcopal Church a vibrant, inspirited set of baptismal practices and understandings. But these practices and understandings differ from those in BCP 1928 and its predecessors. Churchpeople will notice the difference immediately, and these differences, unexplained, can lead to turmoil for pastor and people. The grace of patience, so essential for seeing the church through the first wave of liturgical renewal, becomes even more crucial for the second.

There is a piety accompanying the prevalent attitudes toward baptism in earlier Anglican practice, and it might fairly be characterized as a piety of *salvation.* BCP 1928, for example, names baptism one of the two sacraments "as generally necessary for salvation."[1] BCP 1979, still expressing the primacy of these sacraments of baptism and eucharist, does not refer to them as necessary for salvation but as "the two great sacraments of the Gospel."[2] The current Prayer Book, furthermore, encourages a baptismal piety that might be described as communal and *churchly,* a piety taking the life of the church as a primary point of reference. The opening paragraph from the section, "Concerning the Service," reads:

> Holy Baptism is full initiation by water and the Holy Spirit *into Christ's Body the Church.* The bond which God establishes in Baptism is indissoluble.[3]

---

[1] BCP 1928, 292. The other sacrament is the eucharist.
[2] BCP 1979, 858.
[3] Ibid., 298. Emphasis added.

Baptism in BCP 1979 does not cease to express God's saving action in human life. That is, it does not ask people to abandon a baptismal piety described in terms of salvation. But it does ask people to understand such a piety within a communal context. Baptism forms the church, and the church is its primary expression.[4] The church exists as a sign of God's calling a *people* into salvation with baptism as the sacrament of that call, its tangible expression.[5]

The residue of a baptismal piety expressed chiefly in terms of salvation, however, may put people at odds with this emerging (but also ancient) spirituality expressed mostly in communal terms. The opening rubrical section quoted above differs dramatically from the opening sentence in the rubrics for BCP 1928, which reads:

> The Minister of every Parish shall often admonish the People, that they defer not the Baptism of their Children.[6]

Anglican piety and practice have revolved around this understanding, and often there has been the concern, though seldom articulated, that young children who died unbaptized might not "be saved."[7] Although Anglicanism has shied away from dogma-

---

[4]See Romans 6:1ff.; 12:1ff.; Gal. 3:27–28; Eph. 4:4–6; 1 Peter 2.

[5]See F. D. Maurice, *The Kingdom of Christ or Hints to a Quaker Respecting the Principles, Constitution and Ordinances of the Catholic Church*, 2 vols., 2d ed. (London: SCM, 1958; 2d ed. first published 1842; 1st ed., 1838) for the classic Anglican expression of this communal understanding of baptism.

[6]BCP 1928, 273. A similar rubric in earlier Prayer Books, in the section for private baptism, requires the minister to admonish the people not to defer baptism longer than one or two Sundays after birth. Brightman, *English Rite*, 2:748–49; Marshall, *Prayer Book Parallels*, 1:266.

[7]For contrasting views on this Augustinian understanding of baptism and original sin, see Joseph Hall, *Works* (1837), 6:248ff., in *Anglicanism*, ed. More and Cross, 438–39; and John Bramhall, *A Short Discourse to Sir Henry de Vic about a Passage at this Table, after the Christening of his Daughter, Anne Charlotte, of*

tism on the point of unbaptized children and their destiny,[8] popular attitudes and practices have suggested an underlying anxiety about the fate of a child who might die before baptism. Careful pastors need to attend to this often unarticulated fear that people bring to their consideration of the renewed rites of baptism. The movement into the new understanding, correspondingly, may take years and decades rather than weeks and months, especially when people confront for the first time this idea from *The Book of Occasional Services*:

> In the case of young children, the parents may, in consultation with the pastor of the congregation, determine to defer baptism until the child is old enough to go through the catechumenate.[9]

Such an idea is not out of keeping with a communal or churchly spirituality of baptism, one encouraging the entire household of believers to take a responsibility for preparing people for baptism and helping them to discern God's call in particular circumstances. Herein lies the genius of the catechumenal process, described below. For people whose understanding of baptism emerges from a piety of salvation, however, such an approach might at first seem unfathomable.

For baptism, perhaps more than in any other of the Prayer Book rites, liturgical renewal works best when the understandings are brought to bear incrementally, that is, one step at a time. Perhaps a good first step toward becoming a baptizing community, an identity the Prayer Book encourages, would not be to introduce a full-blown catechumenal process with the possibility of a deferred baptism. A first step toward a communal piety might be

---

Persons Dying without Baptism, in ibid., 439–41.

[8]See, for example, the circumspection in Wheatly, *Rational Illustration*, 7. Appendix 1. 1–2.

[9]*The Book of Occasional Services*, 162.

nothing more complicated or threatening than to have baptisms only at the principal eucharist on Sundays. From that understanding and practice, a fuller baptismal piety, rooted in the experience of the community, can then take shape.

Baptism as Public Worship

"Private baptism" is a contradiction of terms, if we understand baptism as a rite forming Christ's body the church. BCP 1979 does provide for *emergency* baptism,[10] but baptism in dire circumstances, when life is threatened, is not the issue here, for emergency baptism differs markedly from a private rite of convenience or personal preference. The Prayer Book service, furthermore, stipulates a communal "completion" for the emergency baptism, if the person does indeed recover. A full, public rite in the church, in the presence of a priest or bishop, parents, sponsors, and worshiping community, brings the baptized person into the context for understanding his or her baptismal life. A person having received baptism in such extreme circumstances takes part in the entire baptismal service (including the laying on of hands or the anointing with oil) except the water rite. Rebaptism would undermine the ancient credal sensibility of one baptism for the forgiveness of sins, and rebaptism is not the issue. Providing a communal context for celebrating the fullest meaning of baptism is the issue.[11]

The Prayer Book clearly intends the celebration of baptism to take place at the chief eucharist on Sunday or other holy day.[12] This intention, however, derives from the deeper Prayer Book

---

[10]BCP 1979, 313–14.

[11]Ibid. BCP 1928 makes similar provisions. See Marshall, *Prayer Book Parallels*, 1:307.

[12]Ibid., 298.

tradition. BCP 1549 states the norm in the first rubric for the baptismal rite:

> [T]he people are to be admonished, that it is moste conueneint that Baptisme shoulde not be ministred but vpon Sondayes & other holye dayes, when the moste numbre of people may come together. As well for that the congregacion there present maye testifie the receyuing of them, that be newely Baptised, also because in the Baptisme of Infantes, euery manne present may be put in remembraunce of his owne profession made to God in his Baptisme.[13]

Every Prayer Book since has stated this principle in the introductory rubrics to the baptismal service. The very name of the rite in the historic Prayer Books suggests a communal context: "The Administration of Public Baptism To Be Used in the Church."[14] The Prayer Books do provide for "The Ministration of Private Baptism in Houses," as BCP 1662 calls the rite, but such a service is secondary and derivative,[15] only to be used "vpon a great and reasonable cause declared to the curate and by hym approued."[16] Baptism took place after the second lesson at morning prayer or evening prayer (at the priest's discretion).[17] Accordingly, baptisms at the morning service on Sundays or holy days would have taken place in the context of the eucharistic liturgy (morning prayer-litany-eucharist having provided the norm on Sundays and holy days), even if that liturgy stopped short of the liturgy of the table, as was

---

[13]Brightman, *English Rite*, 2:724. Cf. Hooker, *Ecclesiastical Polity*, 5. 59. 1.

[14]See Wheatly, *Rational Illustration*, 7. 1. 1–2.

[15]L'Estrange, *Alliance of Divine Offices*, 275–76.

[16]Brightman, *English Rite*, 2:748. The language comes from BCP 1549, which allowed laypeople to administer baptism in cases of emergency, a function taken away with the increasing clericalism of BCP 1604. This revision restricted baptism to the clergy, a response to the pressure from puritan forces.

[17]Brightman, *English Rite*, 2:726–27; Marshall, *Prayer Book Parallels*, 1:234–25. Only with BCP 1928 is there permission for the priest to exercise the discretion to baptize at some other occasion.

customary with antecommunion. The earliest baptismal practices according to the Prayer Book tradition thus envisioned the rite as belonging to the worshiping community. A private baptism for the sake of convenience or family custom undermines this part of the Prayer Book tradition, so crucial to developing the churchly piety at the heart of the baptismal rite in BCP 1979.

Adult Baptism as the Norm

The rites of baptism in the early church, communal rites all, assumed the baptism of adults as the norm. Infants and young children were baptized also (as were slaves who might have been a part of the household).[18] But the symbolism of a mature man or woman coming to repentance and turning toward Christ, choosing to follow Jesus into the symbolic burial in waters and rising from them, offered the most basic meaning for the sacrament. For the baptism of infants or young children, the church looked to adult baptism for the fullest meaning of the sacrament. The early church effectively transferred the meaning of baptism from its richest expression, found whenever adults were baptized, to all other circumstances. Thus the believers never had to question the validity of infant baptism, for that is not the issue in saying that adult baptism is the norm. In this case, the norm has to do with clarity of meaning. The early church basically expected to baptize adults who came to belief, whose movement through conversion brought a clarity of meaning to the sacrament. From this rich meaning the early church derived its baptismal understandings for infants and young children. Thus in this sense, adult baptism became the *norm* from the outset.

As Christianity became more interwoven with the emerging western culture from the fourth century forward, fewer people

---

[18]See Acts 16:25–34 for a scriptural hint about this practice, usually called "household baptism."

came to conversion during their adult years. Infant baptism became the more ordinary practice, and by the middle ages, adult baptism had become an oddity. The first Prayer Books received this medieval legacy and did nothing to question it, preferring instead to follow the legacy's assumptions about baptizing children. Without fail, the baptismal rubrics in all the Prayer Books before 1979 use "children" or "infants" when describing the candidates for baptism, and the appointed gospel lection from the service comes from Mark 10, Jesus blessing the little children. The intent of the rite was clear. Baptism was for children, and the sooner after birth the better. Only with BCP 1662 is there as much as an acknowledgement that adults might be baptized. In that book we find tucked away after the primary baptismal rite (that is, the one for infants) an order for "The Ministration of Baptism to Such as are of Riper Years, and Able to Answer for Themselves."[19] Clearly this rite, as important as it is in BCP 1662, nonetheless stands in a secondary position to the baptism of infants, still the ordinary means for making Christians in the Church of England.

BCP 1979 does not assume that adult baptisms will outnumber infant baptisms. For now, most congregations will continue to experience infant baptism as the more common expression of the sacrament. But BCP 1979 does place the baptism of adults first in the rite, turning BCP 1662 and its successors around. It gives adult baptism a prominence heretofore unknown in Prayer Book practice. By placing the baptism of infants and young children second, BCP 1979 does not denigrate such baptisms but suggests that their meaning derives from adult baptism. By this subtle repositioning of the elements of the rite, and through the ambiance and intent, BCP 1979 shows that although adult baptism might be the less common expression of the sacrament, it is nonetheless the expres-

---

[19]Brightman, *English Rite*, 2:761.

sion from which the full *meaning* of baptism most clearly flows. Thus adult baptism expresses a norm for baptism, even when a given parish might see such a baptism only once every few years. It provides the standard, the measure, the full significance of turning to Christ, the following of him into the waters signifying death and resurrection.[20] Thus the Prayer Book recovers this baptismal sensibility so common in the life of the early church.

The Catechumenate and the Baptism of Adults

The baptismal rite in BCP 1979 moves the church in the direction of a serious, communal-based preparation for adult baptism called the catechumenate. If indeed adult baptism marks a norm in BCP 1979, it follows that planners need to look seriously at all the implications of such understandings. "A catechumen is defined as an unbaptized adult,"[21] and the catechumenate per se addresses only the unbaptized.

> The catechumenate is a period of training and instruction in Christian understandings about God, human relationships, and the meaning of life, which culminates in the reception of the Sacraments of Christian Initiation.[22]

The Book of Occasional Services, however, does provide additional, parallel rites for the baptized who seek a mechanism for renewing their sense of identity as baptized persons.

As mentioned in Chapter One, the early church developed a lengthy process (up to three years and occasionally longer) to prepare baptismal candidates for life and ministry in a faith that

---

[20]The Catechism in BCP 1979 assumes adult baptism as the norm and shows why children *might* also be baptized. BCP 1979, 858–59.

[21]*The Book of Occasional Services*, 114. The liturgies for the catechumenate and related processes are found in this volume, 114–45.

[22]Ibid.

found itself at odds with many of the ways in the surrounding culture. Such a lengthy catechumenate provided the means for incorporating the candidates fully into the Christian community. And more than that, the Christians' ministry among and with the catechumens—that is, the work of making new Christians—lay at the center of the church's evangelical mission. It was a communal enterprise, involving virtually all the faithful, and it followed closely the seasons of the church year. Baptisms took place at sunrise on Easter day, and the rest of the church year took its shape from that moment.[23] Lent, for example, developed as a season of intensive baptismal preparation, a season of fasting, works of mercy, and prayer first associated with baptismal candidates as they made their final preparation for the sacraments of initiation. The baptismal practices of the church thus came first, and from these the Lenten season took shape. The catechumenal process can help the church towards renewal by recovering these ancient and venerable associations between Lent and baptism, Lent and conversion, Lent and community.

The Book of Occasional Services retrieves these and similar associations and fashions them for contemporary use. For any worship planners seeking to understand the full range of baptismal possibilities, a careful examination of the catechumenate and parallel processes becomes necessary.[24] Here the threads of

---

[23]For an exhaustive treatment of the primacy of Easter in the development of the church year, see Thomas J. Talley, *The Origins of the Liturgical Year* (New York: Pueblo, 1986), 1–70.

[24]The best resource in a single volume is *The Catechumenal Process: Adult Initiation and Formation for Christian Life and Ministry*, ed. Anne E. P. Mc-Elligott (New York: Church Hymnal Corporation, 1990). See also *The Baptismal Mystery and the Catechumenate*, ed. Michael Merriman (New York: Church Hymnal Corporation, 1990) and the materials from the Diocese of Milwaukee, "Living Our Baptismal Covenant: Diocese of Milwaukee" (New York: Episcopal Church Center, 1989).

liturgy, evangelism, church year, social ministry, education, and communal life come together. A parish might examine the materials and even decide against implementing them—but examining the materials could help clarify other important baptismal issues in any parish: Whom do we baptize, and when? Under what circumstances do we baptize? What do we expect from baptismal candidates (or their parents or sponsors)? What can they expect from us? What will preparation for baptism look like? How does this differ from current baptismal practices? How will we shape the baptismal liturgy itself?

Alternatively, the planners for worship could determine that although the catechumenal processes are not currently feasible, such processes help provide a sense of direction for the parish. A parish might reasonably decide "not yet" after its discussions on the catechumenate and find itself the richer for having done so. That "not yet" (instead of the more emphatic "no") could provide a first hint of direction for the baptizing community.

These catechumenal processes draw the church into a more serious consideration of the sacraments of initiation, especially important as we live in cultures increasingly indifferent to matters of belief. No longer will the prescription from BCP 1662 suffice:

> When any such persons, as are of riper years are to be baptized, timely notice shall be given to the Bishop, or whom he shall appoint for that purpose, a week before at the least, by the Parents, or some other discreet persons: that so due care may be taken for their examination, whether they be sufficiently instructed in the principles of the Christian Religion; and that they may be exhorted to prepare themselves with prayers and fasting, for the receiving of this Holy Sacrament.[25]

The cultural situation, no longer at ease with presumptions about Christian believing as a norm, demands more weighty formation of people coming to Christian believing for the first time.

---

[25]BCP 1662, 761.

Baptismal Occasions and the Prayer Book

The rubric at the head of the baptismal order in the first two Prayer Books begins:

> It appeareth by auncient writers, that the Sacrament of Baptisme in the olde tyme was not commōlye ministred but at two tymes in the yeare, at Easter and Whitsontyde, at which tymes it was onenlye ministred in the presence of all the congregacion: Whiche custome (nowe beeyng growen out of use) although it cannot for many consideracions be well restored agayne, yet it is thought good to folowe the same as nere as conueniently maye be:[26]

The rubric does not name the considerations that would keep the practice from being restored,[27] but the point remains that the reformers knew the antiquity of these baptismal feasts from a familiarity with the ancient Christian writers.[28]

Like the first two Prayer Books, BCP 1979 recognizes the antiquity of these baptismal feasts, noting also three other occasions for baptism suggested in the tradition. But, taking the step that BCP 1549 would not, the current Prayer Book actually designates these baptismal feasts as the preferred occasions for baptisms.

> Holy Baptism is especially appropriate at the Easter Vigil, on the Day of Pentecost, on All Saints' Day or the Sunday after All Saints' Day, and on the Feast of the Baptism of our Lord (the First Sunday after the Epiphany).

---

[26]From BCP 1549, in Brightman, *English Rite*, 2:724. The same wording occurs in BCP 1552; BCP 1662 deleted this section.

[27]Hooker, recognizing the antiquity of these baptismal feasts, argues nonetheless that the ancients were perhaps "too severe" in restricting baptisms to two times in the year. Hooker, *Ecclesiastical Polity*, 5. 61.

[28]Wheatly cites evidence about the feasts from Cyprian and Tertullian, noting also the scriptural resonances in Romans 6 (for Easter baptisms) and Acts 2:41 (for Pentecost). Wheatly also knows of the Eastern Orthodox custom of baptizing at Epiphany, and he cites Gregory Nazianzus as evidence. Wheatly, *Rational Illustration*, 7. 1. 1.

It is recommended that, as far as possible, Baptisms be reserved for these occasions or when a bishop is present.[29]

Worship planners, having established Sunday baptisms as the norm, might well consider ways to mark these five primary baptismal occasions. Even if it is not currently possible to have every baptism on one of the baptismal feasts, it might be possible to reserve at least some baptisms for those occasions. An interim step could be to encourage but not force parents, sponsors, and candidates to plan the baptism for one of these dates. The groundwork needs to be laid carefully before the parish can decide that these will be the only occasions (barring emergencies) on which this community will baptize. It is a legitimate decision, one helping the church to understand more fully that communal spirituality assumed in the Prayer Book rite of baptism—but planners should move toward such a policy only with judicious forethought. Even when there can be no baptisms on these feasts, a parish can find a way to mark the occasion. The Prayer Book provides for the option of using the renewal of baptismal vows (from the Easter Vigil) in place of the Nicene Creed as an option on these five days.[30] Planners, choosing this option, could emphasize the baptismal nature of the occasions, even if there are no baptisms to celebrate.

"The Great Vigil of Easter" deserves special attention from worship planners, both for its baptismal associations and for its place in the calendar. The Prayer Book devotes more material to this liturgy than to any other in the yearly cycle. The weightiness of the materials should in themselves suggest something about the importance of this liturgy in the life of the community.

The Easter Vigil gave the early church a feast with three interrelated aspects. First, the vigil celebrated Jesus' resurrection, this

---

[29]BCP 1979, 312.
[30]Ibid.

central mystery in Christian believing and the greatest of God's mighty acts. Second, the vigil celebrated *all* the ways God has acted in Jesus to bring salvation to the cosmos—his incarnation, his life, his death, as well as his resurrection, ascension, and sending of the Spirit; but the vigil also marked all of God's saving acts for the people of God throughout history, now seen anew from the perspective of the resurrection. The bulk of the service consisted of extensive readings from the Hebrew scriptures—the creation, the flood, the sacrifice of Isaac, among others.[31] The crucial passage came with the story of the Exodus and the night of Passover, God's mighty act of liberation from bondage, with the waters of the Red Sea (prefiguring baptism) and the journey to the land of promise. The baptized community celebrated Easter as the *Christian* Passover, a feast in continuity with the one celebrated by God's people of old, a feast of God's mighty acts bringing liberation. Third, the vigil's climax came with the baptism of new Christians, the most recent moment in the story of God's saving acts for humankind and the whole cosmos. The grand panoply of salvation's story fittingly provided the setting for baptism.[32]

BCP 1979 puts all these elements into the Great Vigil of Easter, intending for this service a central place in the church year. It should be the climax of Holy Week, not a mere afterthought. It should also form the most important celebration of Easter. Planners probably cannot immediately shift the emphasis from a late Sunday-morning service, a customary time for the grandest of Easter celebrations, but they can take steps to treat the vigil as the chief celebration of Easter. Publicize it as such. Plan the festive Easter music for the Eucharist concluding the vigil. Encourage and teach the vigil as the baptismal occasion. Let the symbols of light

---

[31]Talley, *Origins of the Liturgical Year*, 2–5, 33–54.

[32]*Hippolytus*, section 21.

and darkness, lengthy readings and silence, water, oil and human touch have their way—and do not undermine them, shorten the readings, or hurry the service. Trust word-of-mouth to have its effect over the course of years.

For the vigil to have its way with us, the readings should be allowed their full force. Here a key is to let go of any need for a cognitive understanding of the readings. There has to be the sense of being overwhelmed by story told in the readings, or else it is not a vigil in the truest sense. Planners need to choose carefully to shape the readings (the more the community will bear, the better), psalms, silences and prayers into a rhythm of leisure, the divine leisure of being washed-over with the story of God's salvation.

It is no mistake that in BCP 1979, the Great Vigil of Easter comes just before the baptismal rite. The two services belong together, each informing the other. Baptism takes its meaning from the mystery of God's acting, especially in the death and resurrection of Jesus. And the Easter Vigil provides the most likely occasion for baptism.

Sacramental Moments as Times for Clarity in Action

Anglicanism has shown an innate trust in the sacraments to convey their own meaning. Classical Anglicanism holds suspect any ceremonial style that obscures the sacramental elements or actions. Timidity of statement with the elements is thus out of place. So baptism, the sacrament whose meaning is revealed in the water, should emphasize the water. The Prayer Book tradition has always noted immersion as the preferred method of baptizing. The pouring of water, although the conventional means of baptizing now, has always been a second choice.[33] Immersion conveys the mean-

[33]Brightman, *English Rite*, 2:740–41; Marshall, *Prayer Book Parallels*, 1 254–55. BCP 1549 stipulated a three-fold immersion, once on the right side, once on the left, and once face forward. All the Prayer Books up to and including the pro-

ing of baptism in a bold, pictorial fashion, like that in Romans 6 —dead in Christ Jesus, buried with him in the waters of baptism, risen to new life out of the waters. The pouring of water, although valid,[34] does not convey the meaning of baptism with such clarity. Baptism is a ritual drowning, and a timid pouring of water does not suggest drowning at all.

The rubrics notwithstanding, immersion as the preferred means of baptism became less common in the latter part of the seventeenth century.[35] Nineteenth-century neo-gothic architecture, furthermore, brought with it a much smaller font than customary in earlier styles and made immersion nearly impossible. Fonts before the gothic revival were at least large enough to accommodate the immersion of an infant, and some were much larger, a style dating from the early church. The neo-gothic fonts, however, provided mere receptacles for the water, as they were much too small for immersing anyone.[36]

---

posed American Book of 1786 allowed for the pouring of water only for a "weak" child.

[34]*Didache*, 7:1–4, in *Ancient Christian Writers: The Works of the Fathers in Translation*, ed. Johannes Quasten and Joseph C. Plumpe, vol. 6, trans. James A. Kleist (Westminster, MD: Newman Press, 1948), 19.

[35]Legg, *English Church Life*, 166–68.

[36]See Chambers, *Divine Worship*, 2. The early tractarians wrote extensively about baptism, stirring up the greatest possible controversy in the process, with Pusey's famous Tract 67, on baptismal regeneration, one of the most controversial works in the whole series. E. B. Pusey, *Scriptural Views of Holy Baptism: As Established by the Consent of the Ancient Church, and Contrasted with the Systems of Modern Schools* (Oxford: J. H. Parker, 1836). See Louis Weil, *Sacraments and Liturgy: The Outward Signs* (Oxford: Basil Blackwell, 1983), 45–49. The ritual movement, however, focused its ceremonial energies almost entirely on the eucharist, with scant regard to baptism. Thus Chambers, exemplifying the early ritualist ideals, devotes a single paragraph of nine lines in a work of 430 pages to the issue of baptism (placement and style of the font), but nine long pages to the design of dalmatics!

Many of our churches, built on the neo-gothic model, have these tiny basins instead of the historic-style fonts designed for immersion. And often in the neo-gothic model, the font is kept in an out-of-the-way corner of the church, not in a central, visible place for the worshiping community. These limitations need to be considered in any remodeling. Planners need also to acknowledge the considerable hesitancy, even anxiety that parents and others might feel regarding the notion of full immersion. They may express a concern about practical issues (Is it safe?), but other concerns come into play also. There is something unsettling about witnessing baptism by immersion, a sheer physicality, a raw quality, almost primal and too immediate. Modest church-goers may find themselves unnerved by such sacramental directness, but it is precisely this sacramental quality that classical Anglicanism trusts: uncover the sacramental riches, with all their unsettling power, and let them speak for themselves.

At the very least, water should be evident and it should be abundant. The sound of its splashing into the basin during the blessing of the water can suggest the physicality of the sacrament. Even when pouring is the only option, immodest amounts of water, scooped up with a bare hand, would be in order. A shell or other vessel for pouring serves only to hold the physical element of human touch at a distance. A good rule of thumb is that the actions at the font should make clear that anyone standing too close would stand in danger of getting wet!

Baptism as Full Sacramental Initiation

The first rubric in the section "Concerning the Service" describes baptism as "full initiation by water and the Holy Spirit,"[37] an

---

[37] BCP 1979, 298.

important point for understanding the baptismal practices in BCP 1979. The earlier Prayer Books suggested the same understanding; the BCP 1979 states it unequivocally, clarifying this understanding from the tradition and bringing it fully into practice.

In the early church, the baptismal rite consisted of three components—the water rite, baptismal anointing with the laying on of hands, and the communion of the newly baptized. When the ancients wrote about baptism, they referred to this entire complex. Over a complicated history, the three components were separated, leaving only the water rite associated with the name baptism.[38] The baptismal anointing and imposition of hands, reserved in the Roman rite (though not in the Eastern or Gallican rite) for the bishop or the bishop's deputy, later was called *confirmation*, although practices varied dramatically from place to place. In some locales, for example, the baptismal anointing had to precede first communion. In other places, first communion remained part of the baptismal rite, even if there would be no baptismal anointing at baptism—or ever.[39]

BCP 1979 makes it possible to celebrate the rite in its restored, threefold integrity. After the water rite, the Prayer Book stipulates that the bishop (who presides if present) or priest impose a hand and mark the sign of the cross on the newly baptized. Chrism, the perfumed baptismal oil blessed by the bishop, may be used with the laying on of hands. BCP 1549 included a baptismal anointing in the rite, but the pressures from the more radical reformers

---

[38]This holds true only for Christianity in the West. In the Christian East, the components never separated. There the rich baptismal liturgy still consists of water rite, anointing, and first communion.

[39]See Charles P. Price, "Rites of Initiation," in *The Occasional Papers of the Standing Liturgical Commission*, Collection Number 1 (New York: Church Hymnal Corporation, 1987), 24–37; and Hatchett, *Commentary on the American Prayer Book*, 251–58, for a more detailed summary of the historical issues.

forced its exclusion from BCP 1552.[40] BCP 1979 recovers this ancient practice. Perfumed oil was associated with the pleasures of the bath in antiquity, and its links with the sacred bath of baptism are well-attested. Christians also cherished baptismal anointing as a sign of their identity with Jesus *the* anointed one, for the Greek word *christos* means literally, "anointed one." Liberal use of oil, its feel on the skin, its sweet odor, its sheen on the forehead, can intensify the physical sense of the sacrament, and planners may want to consider its possibilities and its ancient meanings. Oil in sufficient quantities to be poured from a glass or crockery cruet into the palm of the celebrant (not dabbed from a wad of cotton in one of the "oil stocks" sold by church supply-houses) can be rubbed onto the forehead or crown of the newly baptized. The sign of the cross can then be marked through the oil. An ancient prayer for the gifts of the Spirit, associated with the confirmation rite in earlier Prayer Books, is offered either before or after the anointing (or laying on of hands).

But the Anglican baptismal rite has always included this marking with the sign of the cross after baptism, to the consternation of the puritan forces.[41] It is no innovation in BCP 1979, for Cranmer intended this action from the outset to signify what the *medieval* rite of confirmation had formerly done. That is, he intended the rite to convey a sacramental completeness and to retain a familiar shape.[42] Most of the continental reformers, especially John Calvin, disdained the medieval rite of confirmation as frivolous, extraneous, a human invention; and these reformers dropped the practice from their baptismal rites. Their innovation came with a new rite to celebrate an older child's completing the lengthy catechetical

---

[40]Brightman, *English Rite*, 2:740–43.

[41]Hooker, *Ecclesiastical Polity*, 5. 65.

[42]Hatchett, *Commentary on the American Prayer Book*, 264–65.

courses common in the various traditions of the reformation. This rite consisted of an imposition of hands—and also came to be called confirmation, a cause for confusion ever after. Such a *reformation* rite of confirmation is what Cranmer designed for the Prayer Book service by that name. It is always important to distinguish between the two types of confirmation—medieval and reformation. One is a part of the rites of initiation; the other marks the completion of learning the catechism.[43]

Cranmer's high regard for the Prayer Book confirmation rite (of the reformation type) led him to dignify it by making the bishop the minister of the rite (whereas presbyters were the ordinary ministers in other reformation rites) and by making it a prerequisite for admission to communion. The confirmation rubric, stating this prerequisite, remained in effect through BCP 1928, where it read:

> And there shall none be admitted to the Holy Communion, until such time as he be confirmed, or be ready and desirous to be confirmed.[44]

With such a rubric, Cranmer intended to encourage the learning of the catechism with confirmation to follow. But subsequent history shows mixed results to Cranmer's intent, as detailed in the next section. What he did accomplish, however, was the appearance that confirmation, and not baptism, brought people completely into the life of the church. Even now, Episcopalians commonly though erroneously talk about confirmation, and not baptism, as the sacrament for "joining the church."

BCP 1979 intentionally omits the confirmation rubric, thus

---

[43]Ibid., 260–61.

[44]BCP 1928, 299. Cf. Brightman, *English Rite*, 2:798–99 and Marshall, *Prayer Book Parallels*, 1:436–37, for the subtle differences in successive Prayer Books. The latter clause, "or be ready and desirous to be confirmed," entered the tradition only with BCP 1662.

opening the way for understanding baptism as complete initiation into the church—and as the only prerequisite for communion. First communion, accordingly, may take place as a part of the baptismal rite.[45]

Worship planners need to ask several questions about the shape of the rite. Will all the newly baptized (including infants and young children) receive communion? May parents with scruples refuse to allow their children to be communicated? What mechanics will be used for giving communion to the youngest of infants? When does formal teaching about the eucharist begin for people who have received communion from infancy? And, of no small consequence, how then does confirmation relate to baptism? How can our rite clearly reflect the threefold shape common to baptism in antiquity—and convey that baptism is indeed full initiation into Christ's body the church?

Anglicanism's Love Affair with Confirmation and Confusion about its Meaning

Cranmer unintentionally left Anglicanism a confused legacy surrounding confirmation. After the English restoration (late seventeenth century), the rite received scant attention in the English church, both in theological writings and in pastoral practice. People received communion not because they were confirmed but because they were "willing and desirous" of being confirmed, and thus the confirmation rubric lost its full force because of this qualifying clause added in BCP 1662. In isolated high-church circles and among the non-jurors, confirmation continued to be held in high regard. But its practice was hardly widespread until the nineteenth century, when the tractarians seized the sacrament because of its supposed apostolic origins. With these pressures

---

[45]Hatchett, *Commentary on the American Prayer Book*, 271–72.

and with the rapid expansion of the railroads, English bishops began to take more seriously their diocesan visitations and confirmations. And the rite's popularity grew, with confirmation eventually becoming one of the identifying marks of Anglican practice.[46]

BCP 1979 has clarified expectations about baptismal practices but has left the issue of confirmation clouded. The Prayer Book intends that people be confirmed:

> In the course of their Christian development, those baptized at an early age are expected, when they are ready and have been duly prepared, to make a mature public affirmation of their faith and commitment to the responsibilities of their Baptism and to receive the laying on of hands by the bishop.
>
> Those baptized as adults, unless baptized with laying on of hands by a bishop, are also expected to make a public affirmation of their faith and commitment to the responsibilities of their Baptism in the presence of a bishop and to receive the laying on of hands.[47]

Confirmation in the Prayer Book is not part of the sacrament of initiation, not that imposition of hands disrupted from the threefold rite of baptism.[48] BCP 1979 places the "stand-alone" rite of confirmation (that is, when there are no baptisms) among the Pastoral Offices, not with the baptismal rite. When there are baptisms, the Prayer Book rite places confirmation immediately after the baptisms and baptismal anointing, for confirmation finds its meaning in relationship to baptism. Nonetheless, the Anglican initiation rite is complete in baptism. These are subtle but important distinctions in the Prayer Book rites. Confirmation's

---

[46]See Weil, *Sacraments and Liturgy*, 75–79.

[47]BCP 1979, 412.

[48]To add to the confusion, what Roman Catholics call confirmation *is* the baptismal anointing! Episcopalians need to take care in their dialogues with Roman Catholics around the issue of confirmation—for we are talking about two different (albeit closely related) sets of ritual gestures and ritual meanings.

lineage derives from the reformation-era rite at the end of catechetical instruction. Bishops who use baptismal oil for the laying
on of hands in the confirmation rite only confuse the issue. Although baptismal oil has its place in the Roman rite—and in fact
in that rite it is the sign—nothing in the Prayer Book suggests its
use at confirmation. Indeed, the Prayer Book's structure encourages anointing at baptism but obstructs the use of oil at confirmation.[49]

But confirmation, although not an initiatory rite, does look to
baptism, *the* rite of initiation, for its meaning. Confirmation is a
solemn, public reaffirmation of baptismal promises. And it marks
either a sacrament of maturity (for those baptized in early childhood) or a sacrament of identity (for those baptized adults coming
to the Episcopal Church from another Christian communion).
Planners would do well to make neither more nor less of confirmation than this.

But planners almost always have to deal with the issue of maturity when considering policies for confirmation. What constitutes
maturity in our church and in our culture? Surely in contemporary American culture a twelve-year-old does not embody the
meaning of maturity in any real sense, but how much better em-
bodiment does one find at fourteen? At sixteen? Parents and
parishioners often express anxiety that the church needs to "get
them" (that is, their adolescent children) before they "get away"
and it is too late. These conflicting pressures, often diffuse in
themselves, do little to clarify expectations around confirmation.

---

[49]The baptismal rite has the blessing of the oils just before the water rite. The
confirmation rite, for use when there are no baptisms, contains no form for
blessing the oils. *The Book of Occasional Services* provides for the bishop's
blessing of the oil after the postcommunion prayer, a position in the rite far
removed from any confirmations. BCP 1979, 307; *The Book of Occasional Services,* 234–36.

Let us be clear that confirmation does not land anyone for the church forever, regardless of the age at which confirmation takes place. To expect the rite or preparation for the rite to accomplish such an objective for adolescents is to expect too much. Modest, albeit serious and clearly stated expectations can alleviate some of the anxieties faced by pastor and people. Lionizing an ideal of confirmation classes and treating them apart from the broader range of Christian formation does little to prepare people for Christian living. Sometimes these classes become courses to complete and hurdles to overcome—not structures of support for living a gospel-inspired life. Confirmation marks a way station, not graduation. Planners may want to explore alternative models to prepare candidates for confirmation—including adolescents. Stanley Hauerwas and William H. Willimon describe in detail one possibility (using mentors and an approach of learning-by-doing) in their book, *Resident Aliens*.[50] The insights here fit nicely within the approaches of the catechumenal processes. BCP 1979 frees planners to explore such possibilities, for the Prayer Book no longer assumes the catechism-based (and priest-centered) way of preparing for confirmation as a norm.

Confirmation does not have to be a once-for-all proposition. People may discover a need several times in their life to reaffirm the meaning of baptism, solemnly and publicly, in the presence of the bishop and with the laying on of hands. BCP 1979 provides for such a possibility with the form for reaffirmation.[51] Planners and priests need to take care not to encourage people to decide for reaffirmation lightly or on the spur of the moment. Some criteria

---

[50]Stanley Hauerwas and William H. Willimon, *Resident Aliens: Life in the Christian Colony* (Nashville: Abingdon Press, 1989), 93–111. See also Andrew D. Parker, *Keeping the Promise: A Mentoring Program for Confirmation in the Episcopal Church* (Harrisburg, PA: Morehouse Publishing, 1994).

[51]BCP 1979, 310.

for preparation might be in order, with the understanding that flexibility in the criteria could serve a variety of pastoral needs. The realization that the imposition of hands can be repeated later on could also relieve some of the pressure around "getting" those adolescents before they "get away."

Planners also need an awareness of the sensibilities of adults coming to the Episcopal Church from other communions. Many of them will have already made a mature Christian commitment; others will have been confirmed. Their commitment needs to be honored, both during preparation for the sacrament and when the bishop imposes hands. In more and more dioceses, the form for reception[52] has become the appropriate rite in these situations. It is fitting, nonetheless, for these people to stand with the gathered community and in the presence of the diocese's chief baptismal minister to reaffirm solemnly the meaning of their baptism. The action allows the person to say: "It is in this community and communion of belief that I hope henceforth to explore the deeper meaning of having being claimed by Christ through the waters of baptism." But Christ's claim through baptism remains primary, and our practices when the bishop imposes hands should not suggest that a derivative rite of confirmation (or reception) supersedes the sacrament of the waters.

---

[52]Ibid.

CHAPTER 4

The Eucharist

WHEN ANGLICANS HAVE SET OUT TO WRITE ABOUT the sacraments, their attention has turned naturally to considerations of the eucharist. "Sacramental theology" in the Anglican tradition has mostly meant "eucharistic theology." Nicholas Ridley, Richard Hooker, Lancelot Andrewes, Jeremy Taylor, John Cosin, and Henry Hammond are but some of the most notable theologians from Anglicanism's early and formative era to write extensively about the meaning of the eucharist. The eighteenth-century evangelical John Wesley, often neglected in considerations of Anglican teachings because of his associations with the Methodist movements, remained an Anglican to his dying day and had a high regard for eucharistic worship, about which he wrote at length. These writings and his numerous eucharistic hymns give evidence of the importance Wesley placed on eucharistic practice, which he put at the center of his "method" for Christian living.[1] The nineteenth-century tractarians had a broad-ranging and inclusive sense of sacramental theology (turning, for example, to

---

[1]Crockett, *Eucharist*, 197–215.

such substantive and controversial understandings of baptism as that in Pusey's Tract 67, on baptismal regeneration), but their most exhaustive work came in their writings on the eucharist. And when the tractarians' successors in the ritualist movement focused their energies on the details for a rich ceremonial for the liturgy, they looked most of all at ways to celebrate the eucharist. The neo-gothic architecture designed by the ritualists offered buildings designed for a dramatic celebration of the eucharist—and not much else. In these churches the table is not merely large and centrally placed; its presence is often over-powering. Other liturgical centers (a lectern for the word and a font for baptism, for example) are vastly smaller, not prominently placed, and clearly secondary in importance.

These examples offer evidence for a broad trend: the Anglican tradition has held the celebration of the eucharist in high regard but has not always managed to express this regard in the most helpful ways. From this varied and rich tradition of eucharistic piety, the Episcopal Church has come to shape its primary act of worship. Since the latest round of Prayer Book revision, most Episcopalians have found that going to church on Sunday means an opportunity to celebrate the eucharist, a practice clearly intended by BCP 1979. To quote again that important first paragraph in the section, "Concerning the Service of the Church,"

> The Holy Eucharist, the principal act of Christian worship on the Lord's Day and other major Feasts, and Daily Morning and Evening Prayer, as set forth in this Book, are the regular services appointed for public worship in this Church.[2]

The twin forces of popular liturgical renewal and new scholarly insights, described in Chapter One, have shaped this hard-fought consensus around celebrating the eucharist every Sunday. But

---

[2]BCP 1979, 13.

while these contemporary movements have forced the church to look seriously at the issue of eucharistic celebration, the Episcopal Church derives many of its attitudes and practices from the deeper Anglican heritage. It is a heritage that has expressed a deep reverence for the eucharistic celebration, even during those times when the ordinary Anglican practice has been to celebrate the eucharist only infrequently. This infrequency of celebration, prevalent through most of Anglican history, has never meant a lessening of eucharistic piety. Anglicans have managed to celebrate the eucharist monthly or quarterly or even less frequently and have still maintained an intense and deep regard for the sacrament. We err if we think that infrequent celebration meant that our Anglican forebears had a disregard for the eucharist, for nothing could be farther from the truth.[3] Quirks of history prevented them from the more frequent, weekly celebration that was Cranmer's intent. Liturgical renewal has freed us from those historical quirks, and the stated practice of BCP 1979 gives us the means for fulfilling Cranmer's original hope—a weekly celebration of the eucharist.

The Eucharist as a Means for Transformation of Life

The Anglican reformers of the sixteenth and seventeenth centuries were not concerned so much with the transformation of the bread and wine on the altar as they were with the transformation of the lives of Christian people. The bread and wine of the eucharist had a part to play in this conversion of life, even an unmistakable part ordained by God. But for the reformers, any understanding of the changes in the bread and wine had to come within the context of the changes worked in the lives of believers. Hooker, for example, shies away from writing about a "transubstantiation" in the bread

---

[3]Legg, *English Church Life*, 48–74; Wheatly, *Rational Illustration*, 6. 1. 1–5.

and wine of the eucharist, but he does not hesitate to use that word in regard to what transpires in the lives of the faithful. Through the encounter with the body and blood of Jesus in the sacrament, he writes,

> there ensueth a kind of transubstantiation *in us*, a true change both of soule and bodie, an alteration from death to life.[4]

Hooker holds suspect any understanding of the eucharist tending toward the grossly corporeal, obsessed with Christ's bodily presence in the sacrament. He does maintain, however, that in the bread and wine of the eucharist there is a *real* presence of Christ, but that presence is "mystical" and "instrumental," and he does little to alleviate this ambiguity in terms. He goes on to cite ancient Christian writers (Tertullian, Theodorus, Irenaeus, Cyprian, and Hilary) to prove his point.[5] And he is correct in his surmisal of the ancients' understanding of the eucharist, for they, too, wrote about Christ's mystical (not corporeal) presence. Hooker illustrates one trend in Anglican eucharistic thinking—a willingness to profess *that* Christ is present in the eucharist alongside an unwillingness to explain *how* Christ is present.[6] And sacramental ambiguity, one of Anglicanism's hallmarks when it comes to the eucharist, made its way into the heritage from its beginning. This middle way in eucharistic theology, one focusing on both the transformation of life (primarily) and the transformation in the elements (secondarily) found a bolstering in the Anglican writers of the seventeenth century. Such notables as Andrewes, Taylor, Laud, and Cosin amplified and drew out nuances from Hooker's emphases, but they did nothing to detract from the studied ambiguity

---

[4] Hooker, *Ecclesiastical Polity*, 5. 67. 11. Emphasis added.

[5] Ibid.

[6] L'Estrange, *Alliance of Divine Offices*, 323–24.

typifying the eucharistic theology inherited from the previous generation.[7]

This middle way charted by the reformers avoids two pitfalls, the first having to do with an overly subjective eucharistic piety. A theology claiming transformation of life as a primary purpose can, in an extreme expression, collapse into an unhealthy individualism—that is, an individualism sprung loose from its necessary reference within the life of a believing community. The celebration of the eucharist, concerned as it is with personal lives, nonetheless stands primarily as a communal expression. And properly put, it is the transformation of the community of faith that is at issue. But that subjective, self-referential strand exists in the Anglican tradition, and it goes back to the eucharistic teachings of Thomas Cranmer. The only real presence for Cranmer was that presence effected in the hearts of believers receiving communion. Cranmer taught that this sacramental transformation of heart was even possible entirely apart from the eucharist, the result of an overly subjective and individualistic understanding of communion and its effects. Cranmer thus developed a eucharistic theology effectively (and confusingly) sprung loose from the eucharist itself! The result is that subjective feelings, and not the real and objective elements of bread and wine, came to signify God's acting. Thus for some people following this strain in the heritage, the only "real"

---

[7]Crockett, *Eucharist*, 189–97. See the section entitled "The Eucharistic Presence," in *Anglicanism*, ed. More and Cross, 463–97. Note also the words used for the administration of the bread in BCP 1549, "The body of our Lord Jesus Christ whiche was geuen for thee, preserue thy bodye and soule unto euerlasting lyfe" (emphasizing the objective pole) and the words in BCP 1552, "Take and eate this, in remembraunce that Christe died for the, and fede on him in thy heart by faith, with thankes geuyng" (emphasizing the subjective). BCP 1559 and all subsequent revisions have combined the two phrases to honor both the subjective and objective poles—another sign of ambiguity in Anglican eucharistic practice. Brightman, *English Rite*, 700–1.

eucharistic liturgy is the one that makes them feel a particular way, and without that feeling the eucharist might even be counted as "invalid." The mainstream of classic Anglican teachings, however, shuns this overstated subjectivism.[8]

Likewise the reformers' middle way avoids the problems of an obsession with the bread and wine, the objective elements. The classic Anglican teaching, with its tenacious trust in the middle way for eucharistic teaching, has provided a means for dodging this misunderstanding of the eucharist. Superstitious and magical attitudes toward the eucharist thus have come under suspicion.[9] At times, however, Anglican teachings have found it necessary to emphasize the objective aspects of the eucharist. The tractarians, for example, focused on the eucharist's objective qualities in the hope of clarifying the sacramental fuzziness inherited from the reformers. Even with this emphasis, however, the tractarians (though not all their heirs) took care not to abandon the subjective component. With their avowed tendencies toward the objective pole, the early tractarians claimed only a desire to interpret the deeper Anglican eucharistic teachings and to restate and refocus a eucharistic heritage often encumbered by its many nuances. But these tractarians expressed no desire to abandon the deeper heritage or to ditch its subjective element. They claimed nothing more than a new interpretation to clarify a eucharistic theology they received and cherished from their Anglican forebears.[10]

What implications does this fairly complicated section on theology have for worship planners? In broad terms, it means that

---

[8]Ibid., 164–73.

[9]Articles of Religion, Article XXVIII, "Of the Lord's Supper," BCP 1979, 873.

[10]Weil, *Sacraments and Liturgy*, 52–54. See E. B. Pusey, *The Real Presence of the Body and Blood of Our Lord Jesus Christ: The Doctrine of the English Church* (Oxford: James Parker, 1869), 1–23.

a community's celebration of the eucharist should keep in view both points of reference, the subjective (with the transformation of lives) and the objective (with a focus on the bread and wine). These points of reference can, for example, inform the selection of music. Are we singing too many subjective, personalizing hymns? Or, conversely, do we forget to choose hymnody to express the conversion of life that Anglicanism assumes? These points of reference can also help planners raise questions about ceremonial. Do our gestures and movements suggest an obsession with the elements of bread and wine? Or, conversely, do they suggest a lackadaisical disregard for them? Do they commend the studied ambiguity that marks Anglican eucharistic teaching? Does the ceremonial style honor the presence of the gathered people, or does it have to do entirely with the objective reference? These are basic points of balance that can inform all the planners' conversations as they seek to form the specific shape of eucharistic liturgy in their community.

Understanding the tradition, moreover, can free Anglicans from the tyranny of the subjective. Faithful people thus may celebrate the eucharist without having to fret over every detail of the liturgy for evidence of warmed hearts and excitement. People feeling dull, anxious, or exhausted at the eucharist need not discount their faithfulness, and they need not count the eucharist a "failure" if they leave with the same feelings they brought to the liturgy. On the other hand, the Anglican tradition firmly trusts the eucharist *over the long haul* to transform the life of the faithful community. This long view of changed lives can give perspective to the planners.

Word and Sacrament

Along with subjective and objective emphases in the eucharist, another complementary pair to hold in balance at the eucharist are word and sacrament, for Anglican sacramental theology always assumes a context in the word. This principle, already outlined in Chapter One, bears further elucidation regarding the eucharist.

The liturgy of the word is no mere forethought to the liturgy of the table, a near-negligible component since, after all, it is not "the sacrament." Word deserves as much care as sacrament, for the stately liturgies of the word for Sunday worship in the historic Prayer Books provided the environment from which the liturgy of the table could take its meaning. At the eucharist, word anticipates sacrament; and sacrament depends on word for a context of meaning.[11]

BCP 1979 provides an ample liturgy of the word for the celebration of the eucharist. The three-year lectionary, with three readings and a psalm for each Sunday, over the course of time brings most of the important parts of the Bible into the church's weekly act of worship. The historic eucharistic lectionary, included in Prayer Books through BCP 1928, followed a one-year cycle with two, usually truncated readings. A reading from one of the gospels was always included, and it followed a first reading, ordinarily called "the Epistle" and most often taken from the New Testament writings outside the gospels. Only rarely would a passage from the Hebrew scriptures replace this New Testament reading. The current eucharistic lectionary, in contrast, almost always includes a first reading from the Old Testament or the Apocrypha,[12] a

---

[11] Anthony Sparrow, *A Rationale, or Practical Exposition of the Book of Common Prayer* (London: Charles Rivington, 1722), 156–59.

[12] The only exception comes during Easter season, when the first reading ordinarily comes from the book of Acts, following the pattern in the lectionaries of

second reading from the New Testament, and a gospel reading. Psalms (including the psalm from the lectionary), hymns, or anthems may follow the first two readings, and periods of silence may be kept. And although the rubrics provide the option of omitting one of the first two readings, such an option detracts from the lavishness in the liturgy of the word.[13] "Sermon hymns" have no place in the service, according to the Prayer Book rite, for the rubrics make no provision for music either before or after the sermon, as did earlier Prayer Books.[14] The sermon is assumed to flow from the readings. It should immediately follow the final gospel acclamation, "Praise to you, Lord Christ" (in Rite II). The common practice of preachers praying before or after the sermon[15] likewise disrupts the intended movement in the Prayer Book rite, but an intentional period of silence after the sermon and before the creed could be a reasonable option. Note again that the rite assumes that the liturgy of the word will include a sermon—always.

Earlier Prayer Books provided a fixed form for the intercessions at the eucharist, the familiar prayer "for the whole state of Christ's Church."[16] BCP 1979 adapts that earlier prayer and prints it in the body of the Rite I eucharist, making it the first preference for the

---

the early church. Even here the Prayer Book provides an alternative from the Old Testament.

[13]BCP 1979, 325–26, 357.

[14]This holds true for the ordinary celebration of the parish eucharist on Sundays and other holy days. The Prayer Book *does* require a hymn after the sermon at the ordination of a bishop and for the celebration of new ministry. Such a hymn is optional on Good Friday. BCP 1979, 516, 560, 277.

[15]Sparrow, *Rationale*, 163–64.

[16]Brightman, *English Rite*, 2:663–69; Marshall, *Prayer Book Parallels*, 1:340–45. The exact wording to introduce the prayer varies. BCP 1549 included the intercessory material in the eucharistic prayer proper.

intercessions. Rite II, however, lists six broad headings for material to be included in the intercessions, and the rubrics direct the reader to the six (sample) forms appended to the rite.[17] Rite I also allows these directives as an alternative to the prayer "for the whole state of Christ's Church and the world." Thus BCP 1979 moves away from a single, fixed form for intercessions, the approach of the historic Prayer Books, to suggest other possibilities—an extensive litany (Forms I and V), a shorter litany rather like a series of collects (Form IV), prayers in responsorial style (Forms III and VI), and bidding prayers (Form II). These six forms, sufficient in themselves for the prayers of the people, also provide models to spark the creativity of worship planners. With BCP 1979 parishes have the freedom to amend the given forms and to create new forms of the prayers—even a different form for every Sunday—as long as the prayers include the categories outlined in the directions on page 383, referred to in Rite I, and printed out in the Rite II rubric.[18] The forms in the book should not limit planners, for they can be springboards, suggesting endless possibilities, tapping the creativity of people in the parish to articulate the particular needs of their community.[19]

BCP 1979 is also the first Prayer Book to allow planners to substitute morning or evening prayer for the liturgy of the word at the eucharist.[20] Essentially the daily offices provide an alternative form for this part of the liturgy.[21] This option provides flexibility

---

[17]BCP 1979, 359, 383–93.

[18]BCP 1979, 359.

[19]See Ormonde Plater, *Intercession: A Theological and Practical Guide* (Cambridge, MA: Cowley Publications, 1995), for a splendid attention to crafting the prayers.

[20]BCP 1979, 36, 142.

[21]Note too that An Order of Worship for Evening can introduce a eucharistic celebration. BCP 1979, 112.

for planners and might find a place especially in parishes where Morning Prayer has been an ordinary part of Sunday worship. In such parishes the use of the office for the liturgy of the word can help provide a less difficult transition to weekly eucharist as a norm. Another likely use for morning or evening prayer at the eucharist would be in a parish with a discipline of daily offices, with the eucharist following on one or two of the weekdays. Here the option of using the office for the liturgy of the word allows the community to maintain its shape of daily prayer in the offices without having to double-up with another (and redundant) liturgy of the word for the sake of celebrating the eucharist.

The canticles, often the most-loved parts from morning prayer, can find a place in the eucharistic celebration without the parish having to resort to the office liturgy. The service edition of *The Hymnal 1982* includes a chart suggesting seasonal use of the canticles at the eucharist.[22] There is no reason a canticle could not be used at any point in the liturgy for which the rubrics require or allow a hymn or anthem. But the most likely place for the use of a canticle comes during the entrance rite, where both Rite I and Rite II print the *Gloria in Excelsis*. The Rite II rubric at the heading of the *Gloria* reads,

> When appointed, the following hymn or some other song of praise is sung or said, all standing.[23]

The various canticles fit nicely at this point in the liturgy, and historically they have had specific seasonal associations in the eucharistic rites from Spain, northern Europe, and the East.[24] Careful choices from these canticles can greatly enrich the liturgy

---

[22]Hymnal 1982: Service Music, S355.

[23]Ibid., 356. See 406 for the appointed occasions for using a hymn of praise.

[24]Hatchett, *Commentary on the American Prayer Book*, 321–22.

of the word, especially for those worshiping communities who might never pray the offices.

Many parishes customarily pray morning prayer in the absence of a priest on Sundays, but there is another, more likely alternative for that situation, especially if the norm for Sunday worship is the eucharist. In the Prayer Books until BCP 1892, Sunday worship consisted of morning prayer, litany, and the eucharistic rite, or at least the part that is the liturgy of the word. And although the liturgy of the table might have been celebrated only infrequently, the liturgy of the word proper to the eucharist at least provided a *symbol* of the eucharistic celebration. The practice was not ideal, but it did at least carry some important symbolic value. Might not antecommunion provide such a symbol in parishes accustomed to eucharistic worship, when the priest cannot be there? Could it not remind them, more effectively than does morning prayer, that eucharist and Lord's Day belong together?

The Problematic "Soft Spots" in the Liturgy

Liturgies seem naturally to draw in new materials, and sometimes they grow out of control. A parishioner visits a parish in another state, finds a new idea from the liturgy, and brings it back home, lobbying the priest to implement this wonderful practice. It may in fact be fairly easy to graft such an idea into the liturgy back home. Pruning that graft once it takes hold, however, almost always proves more difficult. Occasionally accretions like these will obscure the basic, classical shape of the liturgy, and thus even the best of ideas for additions to the liturgy deserve careful consideration.

Such new ideas likely will make their way into the eucharistic liturgy at one of three vulnerable points, "soft spots," if you will—the beginning (entrance rite), the middle(at the offertory), and the end (around the dismissal). Corporate devotions at the beginning of the eucharist, for example, are not uncommon, although they are not as prevalent as they once were. Birthday prayers or complicated ceremonials with the money offering often make their way into the liturgy at the offertory. The dismissal may mark a time of general confusion, not infrequently with a ritualized extinguishing of the candles and even a hymn after the dismissal. Planners need to beware of extraneous actions that might confuse the basic flow of the liturgy.

But planners need to attend to these three points not simply because they attract confusing accretions. These points in the liturgy *already* are weighted down with options, and careful choices from these options are in order. Historically the rites have grown from a reasonable simplicity into something more complicated and ragged at these three points. Thus, for example, the early Roman rite began the liturgy with the entrance of the ministers (in silence) and a collect. And that was it. The readings then followed this unencumbered form for the part of the liturgy technically called the entrance rite. From that simple, straightforward shape, the entrance rite has grown. The readings still follow the collect in Prayer Book usage, but before the collect all or some of the following might come: an entrance hymn, a penitential order (with or without the decalogue, with or without a sentence from scripture), an opening acclamation, the collect for purity, the *Gloria in Excelsis* or some other hymn when appointed, or else a *Kyrie* or *Trisagion*. And *finally* comes the collect. Rite I also allows for the summary of the law or Ten Commandments, even when there is no penitential order. And that rite provides the option of using the *Gloria* and *Kyrie* (or *Trisagion*) in one service![25] Although differing greatly in details, the basic pattern shaping the entrance rite in BCP 1979 does not diverge markedly from that in the historic

[25]BCP 1979, 317–25, 350–56.

Prayer Books.[26] There is, however, one important difference, in that the current Prayer Book makes provision for choices among most of these elements. And here the work of planners becomes important, for they need to know what is required and what is optional. One way of celebrating a Sunday in Lent might include beginning with an entrance hymn with Lenten themes, a full penitential order with the decalogue, a pensive and complex *Trisagion*, and the collect. A lengthy entrance rite like this has its place and can form one means for keeping a Sunday in a peniten-tial season. Another legitimate way to shape an entrance rite during Lent, however, might be for the ministers to enter in si-lence, go immediately to the penitential acclamation, move to a simple *Kyrie*, and conclude with the collect. A stripped-down entrance rite like this can also express a penitential sensibility, for obvious simplicity and starkness may draw attention as well as do elements added-on. Planners need to know their way through this part of the liturgy and all its options.

Similar choices come in the section following communion. A hymn may come before or after the postcommunion prayer (not both), after which comes the blessing and/or the dismissal. Note that Rite I requires a blessing, with the dismissal as an option; Rite II requires a dismissal, with the blessing as an option. After this the people are free to leave. Excessive or ill-placed music, fussy and extraneous ceremonial, and careless choices for the shape of the dismissal can result in confusion.[27]

The offertory marks the third soft spot in the liturgy. Gathering the offerings of bread, wine, and money seems to attract a disorder in movement and confusion in meaning. Usually the simplest,

---

[26]See Brightman, *English Rite*, 2:638–47; and Marshall, *Prayer Book Parallels*, 1:312–25.

[27]BCP 1979, 339–40, 366.

most straightforward way of getting the gifts to the altar will prove the best, but fine-tuning the movements will often tax the abilities of worship planners. The gifts do not have to pass from usher to acolyte to deacon to celebrant back to acolyte, for the bearers of the gifts can hand them directly to the deacon or priest. A hymn, psalm, or anthem is optional, as are the offertory sentences from scripture. But the Prayer Book makes no provision for the celebrant to say, "This holy eucharist is offered to the Glory of God and with special intention for . . . ." The Prayers of the People, not the priest's words paraphrased from the Roman rite, provide the occasion for intercession in BCP 1979.[28]

These three moments in the liturgy—beginning, middle, and end—all involve movement. Planners need to consider the complications that movement can bring as they weigh the various options in the rites. Planners should also recognize that most efforts of liturgical reform (including Cranmer's) involve simplification of the liturgy at these three points. Contrary to some popular attitudes, real liturgical reform seldom results from adding on. It usually comes with paring down, so the great symbols and gestures esteemed by the tradition can take the prominence they deserve.

The Shape of the Liturgy: A Pattern to Honor

Gregory Dix's greatest contribution in his magisterial (although occasionally fanciful) work, *The Shape of the Liturgy*, came with his naming the basic actions at the liturgy of the table: *taking* (the offertory and preparation of the table), *blessing* (the eucharistic prayer), *breaking* (preparing the one loaf for communion by

---

[28]BCP 1979, 333, 361.

breaking it into sufficient pieces), and *sharing* (the communion of the faithful). Dix's work, derived from his study of ancient liturgies, directly influenced the flood of eucharistic liturgies from the 1950s forward—Anglican, Roman Catholic, Lutheran, and Methodist, to name a few of the communions whose reformed eucharistic celebrations have looked to Dix for insights.

For Episcopalians Dix's work brought two important changes in the liturgy, clarifying its shape. First, the historic Prayer Books put the preparation of the table with the collection of alms just before the intercessions—the prayer "for the whole state of Christ's Church," as BCP 1928 put it.[29] BCP 1979 restores these actions to their classical position in the shape of the liturgy, just before the eucharistic prayer.[30] Second, the Prayer Book rubrics from BCP 1662 forward had the breaking of the bread during the eucharistic prayer, with the fraction accompanying the rehearsal of Jesus' actions with the bread:

> [I]n the same night that he was betrayed [Jesus] took bread, and when he had given thanks, he brake it, and gave it to his disciples.[31]

At the words, "he brake it," the rubrics told the priest to break the eucharistic bread into pieces for communion.[32] BCP 1979 moves the breaking of the bread from the eucharistic prayer to its classical position just before the communion of the people.[33] Thus no longer does the eucharistic liturgy meld the breaking of the bread

---

[29]Brightman, *English Rite*, 2:662–63; and Marshall, *Prayer Book Parallels*, 1:340–41.

[30]BCP 1979, 333, 361.

[31]From BCP 1662, in Brightman, *English Rite*, 2:693.

[32]Wheatly explicitly notes the usual practice of breaking the loaf into sufficient pieces for communion, contrasted with the ritual breaking of the single "priest's host" in the Roman rite. Wheatly, *Rational Illustration*, 6. 22. 2.

[33]BCP 1979, 337, 364.

into the eucharistic prayer. BCP 1979 distinguishes *breaking* from *blessing*.

The Prayer Book assumes that planners will understand the classical shape of the liturgy and will undertake strategies to keep the actions distinct and balanced. The offertory, for example, needs to involve a distinct action with representatives of the people gathering the money offering and bringing the gifts of bread, wine, and money to the altar. Directness of action expresses a sense of *offering* that excessive ceremonial often obscures.

The demeanor of the celebrant at the eucharistic prayer—and the ceremonial style used—can invite the people into the act of blessing, or it can exclude them. A very busy presider can suggest that the act of eucharistic blessing is his or hers alone, and accordingly a priest should consider carefully what every gesture, manipulation, sign of the cross, solemn bow and genuflection might communicate. In the Prayer Book tradition a sense of ceremonial reserve has marked the eucharistic rites in general and the eucharistic prayer in particular.[34] The only gesture required for the eucharistic prayers in BCP 1979 is that the celebrant touch or hold the bread and wine at the words of Jesus.[35] Most celebrants will want to pray with uplifted hands (a traditional posture) and extend hands over the bread and wine or make the sign of the cross at the invocation of the Spirit (the epiclesis). But gestures beyond these, while not out of the question, always beg the most careful consideration.

Eucharistic ceremonial often hurries past a significant action at

---

[34]Contrast the rubrics in BCP 1549 and BCP 1552 with the ceremonial associated with such late medieval rites as found in the books of Sarum to understand Cranmer's rule of simplicity and directness at the Lord's table. Brightman, *English Rite*, 2:383–722.

[35]See the pertinent rubric in Prayer 1 and Prayer A, for example, BCP 1979, 334, 362.

the breaking of the bread. The use of loaf bread, a likely choice both from the tradition and from the sensibilities of the current Prayer Book, helps convey the full meaning of this moment, technically called "the fraction." The one loaf is broken into many pieces, so the various members of the one body that is the church may share in the body of Christ. BCP 1549 describes the bread for the eucharist as

> unleavened and rounde, as it was afore, but without all maner of prīte, and some thing more larger and thicker than it was, so that it may be aptly deuided in diuers pieces: and every one shalbe deuided in two pieces, at the leaste, or more, by the discrecion of the minister, and so distrubuted. And men must not think less to be receiued in parte, then in the whole, but in eche of them the whole body of our sauioure Iesu Christe.[36]

BCP 1662, following the change in BCP 1552, assumes that ordinary loaf bread of the sort likely to be found at mealtime will be used for the eucharist.[37]

The breaking of the bread and the pouring from the flagon (for additional chalices)—in silence or with an anthem, with a single loaf or with wafers—deserves high relief and should not be hurried over. The action of breaking and pouring should be evident to the gathered community. Other presbyters (and deacons) stepping forward to the table to join the work, as the Prayer Book suggests, helps draw attention to this important moment.

Planners need to arrange for a communion time that does not take longer than the other three elements of the shape combined. Again, a sense of balance makes it possible for planners to understand the requirements of the liturgy. Sufficient communion ministers helps this action to flow smoothly.[38] Additional commu-

---

[36]BCP 1549, in Brightman, *English Rite*, 2:716.

[37]Brightman, *English Rite*, 2:717.

[38]Note the pertinent rubric, BCP 1979, 408.

nion stations may be necessary when planners expect large crowds. The individualistic piety around communion has often encouraged an excessive lingering at this point, but planners and people alike may need to remember that one ancient sensibility describes communion as "food for the journey," a holy meal for a people eager to get on to the next moment of life and ministry.

Finally, planners can consider ways to keep some other elements of the liturgy from overwhelming this basic shape. The "soft spots" in the liturgy, described above, note three points in particular that, left unchecked, can detract from the clarity of the four-fold shape. The clearing of the table, for example, an action toward the end of the liturgy, does not deserve more intricacies and attention than those required for the preparing of the table. The rubric provides reverent but uncomplicated options for handling any consecrated bread and wine left after the communion of the people.[39] An understanding of proportionality can suggest the ceremonial for this moment in the liturgy—and others like it.

Six Eucharistic Prayers

Each of the earlier Prayer Books contained but a single eucharistic prayer, formed by the rearranging of Cranmerian ideas(as described in Chapter One) and clearly within that heritage. The single eucharistic prayer had the advantage of bringing a uniformity of practice in Prayer Book usage, although such diverse groups as the non-jurors and the tractarians found the liberty to experiment with other styles of eucharistic praying. The liturgical movement in this century, bolstered by scholarly insight, has led to a desire for multiple expressions in eucharistic praying rather than the single expression in previous Prayer Books. Thus BCP

[39]BCP 1979, 408.

1979 offers six eucharistic prayers, two in Rite I and four in Rite II—with an additional two prayers in skeleton form for "An Order for Celebrating the Holy Eucharist."[40] Planners must choose among these options.

Prayer I of Rite I is essentially the latest revision from the work of non-juring Scots as adapted for American usage. It is the traditional eucharistic prayer for the American church, unchanged in substance since 1789. The prayer retains some aspects of Cranmerian theology but represents a substantial reshaping of Cranmerian elements along lines foreign to the first reformers. Although the prayer most familiar to many Episcopalians from their experience prior to Prayer Book revision, Prayer I has some deficiencies, notably a treatment of the incarnation that focuses almost entirely on Jesus' crucifixion and an omission of praise to God for creation. Prayer II of Rite I is a completely reworked version of a prayer in traditional language, preserving some of the familiar Cranmerian phrases but rectifying some of the inadequacies in a traditional prayer like Prayer I. Thus for many planners Prayer II might become the prayer of choice for Rite I, for it keeps some of the treasured phrasing from earlier prayers but enriches the scope of eucharistic praying, following the sensibilities of the ancients.[41]

Prayer A of Rite II offers an attempt to express in modern idiom a prayer following the main currents of Anglican eucharistic theology. Thus, for example, Jesus' atoning death on the cross finds a central place in this prayer. Prayer B translates and adapts the eucharistic prayer of Hippolytus, a prayer from third-century Rome. This revision modifies Hippolytus' structure to include

---

[40]The latter is found in BCP 1979, 400–5, The rubric on 405 states: "[This service] is not intended for use at the principal Sunday or weekly celebration of the Holy Eucharist."

[41]Hatchett, *Commentary on the American Prayer Book*, 359–74.

proper prefaces and a sanctus (lacking in the original) to fit a contemporary and recognizably Anglican setting. The prayer emphasizes God's word in the history of salvation and God's word incarnate in Jesus. Prayer C offers the boldest composition in BCP 1979, drawing on modern, existential images, using many and varied congregational responses, and forming a prayer structured after a model not common in traditional Anglican usage.[42] Although the language and imagery in Prayer C, oddly penitential in tone, may help many of the faithful sense a poetic relevancy to their eucharistic praying, it has the disadvantage of making people more bound to the book than desirable(because of the many and varied responses). Many celebrants also find the unusual structure of the prayer awkward. Prayer D, the last of the revised prayers, is an abridged translation of an ancient prayer still used in Eastern Orthodoxy, the Prayer of St. Basil the Great. It is the most immodest and expansive of all the prayers in its praise of God.[43]

Worship planners can find creative ways to choose the eucharistic prayer for the occasion. Many communities will want to key the prayers to the seasons of the church year, choosing, for example, Prayer C (with its penitential tone) for Lent, Prayer B (with its emphasis on the incarnation of God's word) for Advent and Christmas, and Prayer D (effusive in praise) for Easter. Planners need, however, to avoid the rigidity of considering any of these prayers as one-dimensional expressions. Thus it is not correct glibly to say, "Prayer C is the only penitential prayer" or "Prayer B is the only right choice for Advent and Christmas." There are other legitimate choices. Some communities, having a deep famil-

---

[42]This prayer, with a split epiclesis, follows the structure found in the ancient Alexandrian and Roman rites, not the West Syrian rites which form the usual pattern for Anglican eucharistic prayers in non-juring, Scottish, and American traditions.

[43]Hatchett, *Commentary on the American Prayer Book*, 374–78.

iarity with all the prayers, might also look to the lectionary to help for insights in selecting a prayer. Such communities might feel more comfortable changing eucharistic prayers more frequently than with the season and could even bear a different prayer every week. Caution is in order, however, and switching between Rite I and Rite II from week to week is not advisable.

A Eucharistic Ambiance: Communal and Celebratory

The Prayer Book tradition has presumed that the eucharistic celebration would take place in and give life to a community. BCP 1552, for example, reads:

> And there shalbe no celebracion of the lordes Supper excepte there bee a good noumbre to communicate wyth the priest, accordynge to hys discrecion.
>
> And yf there be not aboue twentie persons in the Parishe, of discrecion to receyue the Communion: yet there shalbe no Communion, excepte foure, or three at the least communicate wyth the prieste.[44]

The Prayer Book rationale for shaping a liturgy to serve priest and people demanded participation from all the faithful. And thus BCP 1549 moved away from a late medieval piety that had the people gathering to *observe* the liturgy, for Cranmer's ideal had people gathering to *join in* the liturgy. BCP 1552 and subsequent books have built on this understanding, drawing the people more fully into liturgical participation. At the *Kyrie*, for example, BCP 1549 has the "Clearkes" (but not the people) singing the familiar hymn that begins "Lorde haue mercie vpon us." BCP 1552, expanding the *Kyrie* into what is called a "trope," intertwines the

---

[44]BCP 1552, in Brightman, *English Rite*, 2: 715. See Wheatly, *Rational Illustration*, 6. 30. 4. Some Elizabethan Injunctions interpret this not as a minimum number (four or three) but as a minimum proportion of a congregation necessary (four or three *out of twenty*).

response "Lorde haue mercy vpon us, and encline our heartes to kepe thys lawe" with all ten of the commandments from the decalogue. The rubric has the people making the response, as has been the case in subsequent Prayer Books.[45]

BCP 1979 continues the process of making Anglican liturgy a work of priest and people. Not only does this Prayer Book draw the people into parts formerly reserved for the priest,[46] but more importantly, the ambiance of the rites is that of God's people gathering around the table.

The current Prayer Book also delineates clearly an expectation for a multiplicity of ministries—bishops, priests, deacons, and laypeople—in the liturgy. Careful reading of the rubrics tells which order has the responsibility for doing what, and who might substitute for the various functions in the absence of a person in the preferred order. Here is an intentional movement toward a more communal celebration than that found in earlier Prayer Books, which essentially allowed a one-person show for the eucharistic celebration. BCP 1549, for example, assumes that other "clearkes" will assist in the eucharist, but a telling rubric reads: "When there are no clearkes, there the Priest shall saye all things appointed here for them to syng."[47] This sensibility, with minor

---

[45]Brightman, *English Rite*, 2:641–43. But note that when the 1549 *Kyrie* re-entered the tradition as an option to the troped *Kyrie* and ten commandments in BCP 1892, the rubric introducing the *Kyrie* reads: "Here, if the Decalogue hath been omitted, shall be said . . . " The passive voice in the rubric does not state who will do the saying; thus priest, choir, or people might legitimately take the part. The passive-voice rubric remains in effect in BCP 1979. Marshall, *Prayer Book Parallels*, 1:320–21.

[46]See, for example, the option for the people to join the priest in saying the (now optional) Prayer of Humble Access and the postcommunion prayer in Rite I, and the stipulation that priest and people say together one of the two postcommunion prayers in Rite II. Marshall, *Prayer Book Parallels*, 1:369, 372–75.

[47]Brightman, *English Rite*, 2:710.

changes, continued through BCP 1928. The current Prayer Book marks an all-important shift in attitudes and for the first time assumes that the laity (and not "the clearkes") take precedence for some of these ministries.

Cranmer, like other reformers both in England and on the continent, regarded the liturgy as an occasion for teaching. He found in the eucharist a special opportunity for instructing the gathered people about their sinfulness and lack of worth. Even a cursory glance at his eucharistic rites will show a heavily didactic and penitential ambiance—exhortations, a troped decalogue, a mournful confession of sin, the Prayer of Humble Access, interspersions of scripture (and those mostly about sin), even a eucharistic prayer that mostly addresses issues of human sinfulness. Subsequent revisions mitigated some of the heaviness in the rite, but even these retained a distinct ambiance of penitence. As noted in Chapter Two, the eucharist (from the Greek *eucharistia*, thanksgiving) often gave people scarce opportunity for thankfulness and did not seem celebratory at all.

BCP 1979 turns to the ancient sensibility of eucharistic celebration—not penitence—for its chief expression. This sensibility becomes especially evident in Rite II. It is possible to make choices that would shape the Rite I eucharist into a heavily didactic and penitential service akin to that in the earlier Prayer Books. But it is also possible to make choices (and permissible omissions) to shape Rite I into a genuine celebration. Indeed, the phrase *communal celebration* summarizes the current Prayer Book's intent for the eucharist. The phrase can become a mantra for worship planners, one to help them form an appropriate ambiance for eucharist. The phrase challenges them to take care in choosing hymns and other music appropriate to support such an ambiance. It questions every nuance of ceremonial and movement. It asks the presiders in liturgy to take into account their personal bearing and how it affects the entire community. Considerations of personal affect and its influence on the community bring a difficult set of issues to ordained ministers, challenges for their developing spirituality. The norm of communal celebration raises issues about architecture and setting. Does the architecture or some fixture in it suggest heaviness? Does it remove the people from the main action or from one another? What do physical barriers (steps, rails, long distances) between priest and people say about the communal quality of the celebration?

The eucharistic celebration does not have to be all lightness, and indeed the Prayer Book provides for a penitential *celebration* of God's forgiveness to sinners. The penitential orders, options for beginning the two rites, present opportunities for penitential occasions. They are not appropriate all the time, but they do have their place in the cycle of the church year. Congregations also need to sing hymns in the minor key, not just hymns in G major, to express the deeper yearnings of the soul, yearnings that sometimes have to do with sin—but sometimes the yearnings have to do more with an odd quality of joy that is inexpressible in any other mode.

Worship planners should assume that every choice about the liturgy makes a difference. The current Prayer Book clearly points in one direction when it comes to eucharistic celebration. But here especially, the book demands that planners enter the discussion, for the choices presented are many.

CHAPTER 5

The Pastoral Offices

THE TWELVE SERVICES CALLED "PASTORAL OFFICES" in BCP 1979[1] suggest unique opportunities in the life of a worshiping community, for these liturgies allow believers to ponder and celebrate the meaning of various life passages. These services mark moments of crisis common to the human experience. Personal crisis often demands pastoral attention, but in appropriate circumstances and with sensitive handling, the crisis may also come to have a place in enriching the life of the community. Christian believing, reflected in its rites of worship, affirms that there is interplay between the personal and the communal. Terms like "pastoral" and "crisis" attract misunderstanding, so some explanations are in order. "Pastoral" is not limited to the

---

[1]Confirmation, A Form of Commitment to Christian Service, Celebration and Blessing of a Marriage, The Blessing of a Civil Marriage, An Order for Marriage, Thanksgiving for the Birth or Adoption of a Child, Reconciliation of a Penitent, Ministration to the Sick, Ministration at the Time of Death, Burial of the Dead: Rite One, Burial of the Dead: Rite Two, and An Order for Burial. The Pastoral Offices are found in BCP 1979, 411–507. This chapter deals with all the offices except confirmation, discussed at length in Chapter Three in its associations with baptism.

private or narrowly personal, as it is sometimes treated. It has a broader context and meaning. A priest who limits pastoral care to dealings with isolated individuals and their needs misses the threads that link persons with one another. Pastoral care requires a vision broad enough to consider how the community is affected by (and becomes a resource for) its separate parts. The pastoral offices, properly used, can provide one structure to encourage pastors and their communities to maintain that broad vision.

"Crisis," often taken only in its negative connotations, here refers to a period in life, brief or extended, that is so rich in possibilities or so fraught with dangers—or both—that life is never the same afterward. Passing through the crisis brings a change, often experienced as conversion. If the period has indeed been a crisis, then the person afterward will discover that life can never be the same again. Life-threatening illness, for example, represents one kind of crisis. The resolution of the crisis comes with recovery—or with death. Christian believers learn that either way, death or recovery, can properly express a kind of conversion, for death in many instances becomes a final healing. Not only that, but Christians learn to profess that the crisis of death finds resolution in the new life of resurrection, life's final conversion.

Persons encountering these life-crises are often vulnerable to outside forces, for the issues of the crisis can consume all their energies. A seriously ill person, for example, may have to confront pain, exhausting therapies, thoughts of mortality, family anxieties, and financial uncertainty. A faith community's ministry of caring for those who are ill or infirm can support these persons through their vulnerabilities. The various means of support can also help people in crisis retain enough of their energies to attend to the stirrings of God, an important issue for believers. A life-crisis, however, does not have to be charged only with these negative understandings. A man and woman entering marriage, for example, are also vulnerable to the forces around them, for they likewise find their energies focused on a life-changing period in their life. Their experience of crisis, however, may point them more clearly toward hopeful possibilities. Yet even the making of the covenant of marriage is not without risk.

The Christian experience of these life-crises often testifies to an inexplicable presence of the divine. These are Spirit-rich times. People passing through life-crises may testify, then or later, to God's working, perhaps incomprehensibly, during such strange times. Friends and family may also learn to make a similar witness. People going through these passages, and their fellow-travelers, do find themselves vulnerable to outside forces. It is not unlikely that the passages should leave people vulnerable to the working of God.

The various pastoral offices in the Prayer Book give ritual expression to the support a faith community has to offer to persons in crisis. More important, these liturgies proclaim the presence of God in the life-changing moment. A personal awareness of God at the time, however, is not necessarily the point of celebrating the rites, nor is that awareness a prerequisite. A seriously ill person, for example, may welcome a ritual assurance of God's presence and healing power, for such assurance may express a presence he or she has already recognized. But another person may find illness a time of experiencing God's absence, a time of depression and desolation. The liturgies for the sick do not discriminate and say that only those who have the "right kind" of experience or feeling or understanding deserve the ministrations. The liturgies for the sick dare to proclaim a divine and healing presence even when the illness draws all those involved—the person who is ill, family, friends, physicians, priest, community—into desperation and a Job-like questioning of God's presence and purpose. These rites even proclaim the power of healing in the face of death itself, for the full meaning of healing goes beyond describing a mere cure. Similarly, the rites of reconciliation proclaim God's forgiving presence, even when such forgiveness feels unlikely in the life of the penitent. Likewise the marriage rites proclaim a divine presence, even when the conscious energies of the man and woman are so intensely drawn to each other and to the festivities of the moment that the mention of God seems superfluous.

All the pastoral offices help bring resolution to the life-crisis presenting itself, and they do so by offering a communal voice, and an honest voice, to the situation. The communal language in the burial rites, for example, speaks with such frankness about death that some worshipers are left feeling uncomfortable through their encounter with the words. The rites for the dead in the Prayer Book do not try to deny death's reality. They instead name death for what it is and honor its presence. Such ritual honesty begins the movement toward resolution in the crisis of grief. A frank acknowledgment of death, as painful as it can be for families and friends at the moment, is a crucial element for their ability to move through the crisis of death and grieving. Persons on their own may not be able find the words for such acknowledgment, so the words of the community in the burial rites give them a voice. The burial rites also speak clearly about death as conversion, that final conversion called resurrection. Thus they bespeak a hopeful realism. But the pathway for that conversion to new life comes only through the crisis of death, life's final change.

In similar fashion the Prayer Book makes it possible for persons to express their sins honestly, even bluntly (in the rites of reconciliation), to acknowledge the crisis of illness head-on (in the rites for the sick), to admit that death is at hand when that is the case, to celebrate and to name the joys and trials of living in the covenant of marriage. When the voice of the individual proves inadequate, then the voice of the community in its rites fills the void.

The Personal and Communal in the Pastoral Offices

This juncture between the personal and communal in the pastoral offices offers opportunities for a worshiping community. The rites acknowledge the turning points in the life of individual persons, and they look to the community as the context for discovering meaning and uncovering the resources for support. The heritage of scripture and the tradition of worship belonging to the community suggest possible points of reference for the individual. Careful pastors cultivate a sensitivity to those points at which the story of individual believers and the story of the Christian heritage of believing come together. The pastoral offices provide some of the most likely occasions for a community of faith to mark these intersections.

But this juncture between the personal and the communal also marks the most difficult aspect of the pastoral offices for pastors and other worship planners. Personal and communal issues often come together to stake out a point of tension, even turmoil. Persons at one of these life-crises may argue against and even reject the community's voice, preferring instead their own voice, even if it is an isolated one or thoroughly idiosyncratic. The North American experience fosters a strong, opinionated individualism, often touted as a cultural virtue in popular lore and understanding. This lore celebrates the idiosyncratic. Such insistent individualism, however, often comes at cross-purposes when it encounters a way of believing that looks to life in community as its primary point of reference. Pastoral Anglicanism is not individualistic but thoroughly *personalistic*—that is, concerned primarily with the life of persons-in-community. According to this pastoral outlook, community provides the necessary context for the care and nurture of persons. Community is not incidental to the pastoral enterprise. This approach to pastoral care, however, often runs counter to the expectations of people formed by the culture of individualism. Even so, pastoral Anglicanism is not individualistic, at least not in the sense that would set the person *against* community or have the person treat community as ancillary or beside the point, as is the case in much of the North American lore and understanding. Often the pastoral approach of Anglicanism (personalistic) comes at odds with the expectations of the popular culture (individualistic). These junctures between the personal and the communal in the pastoral offices can become battlegrounds for conflict. Weddings in particular can provide the occasions for pastoral Anglicanism and popular North American culture to come in conflict, for these two cultures claim different presuppositions and approaches to an important life passage.

This pastoral tack common to Anglicanism, the nurture of persons-in-community, offers a first liturgical principle for the pastoral offices. Any consideration of the pastoral offices requires a treatment of two poles, the personal and the communal. Planners can learn to hold these in creative tension, as complements, and not as two sides always in conflict. The rites allow and even demand that adequate expression be given to both elements—but each in its place. And the Prayer Book tradition quietly asserts that the personal voice usually finds its most adequate expression in the words of the community. Many planners will want to draft customaries or guidelines for some or most of the pastoral offices to state communal expectations and their importance. These guidelines need, on the one hand, to state clearly and succinctly the norms of the community; on the other hand, guidelines and customaries need a certain suppleness, perhaps even a studied ambiguity at points, lest the statement of communal expectations lapse into an unintentionally harsh legalism.[2] Attempts at con-

---

[2]See the subsection, "The Prayer Book Way as *Via Media*," in Chapter One,

sensus, at least among the leadership (including planners and vestry), seeking to spell out what is important and what is not, with clarity and concision in statement, will usually result in a set of communal guidelines that people can honor and find helpful.

Nonetheless, every one of the pastoral offices has a communal point of reference, and planners drafting a customary should not hedge in articulating their communal understandings. These understandings are implicit in the rites and historical practices.

The Personal and Communal in the Various Pastoral Offices of the Tradition

BCP 1549 and BCP 1552 limited the solemnization of a marriage to Sundays and other holy days, when it would take its place after morning prayer and the litany and before the eucharist in the usual routine of the community's worship. These early Prayer Books also required the newly married couple to receive communion in the context of that worship. They were to be active, participatory members—communicants—of the worshiping community. The requirement for publishing banns before the marriage also drew the community's attention to the forthcoming union and re-emphasized that marriage is not merely a private matter between two people and never clandestine.[3] These early rites thus maintained a rich communal ambiance for the celebration of marriage. But gradually this full communal rite eroded into that truncated service familiar in the American Prayer Book tradition from BCP 1789 through BCP 1928. This strain of the Prayer Book

---

above, 26. The same moderate principles behind Prayer Book rubrics can inform a parish's statement of expectations for the pastoral offices.

[3]Wheatly, *Rational Illustration*, 10. 2. 1.; and Hatchett, *Commentary on the American Prayer Book*, 429. See Brightman, *English Rite*, 2:800–1.

lineage preserved materials that the early Prayer Books had assumed would find their place during Sunday worship whenever there was a wedding. These later adaptations, however, set the materials for weddings apart from Sunday worship. The tradition thus lost the norm for a communal setting, and weddings frequently took on a quasi-private ambiance avoided in the early rites.[4] BCP 1979 reasserts the communal aspects of the marriage rite[5] and assumes that a wedding is primarily an act of worship, taking its shape around a liturgy of the word and (ordinarily) a liturgy of the table. The rite leaves open the possibility that weddings can take place at the Sunday eucharist; it does not require it. Implicit, however, is an understanding that the Sunday norm of word and table gives the marriage rite its basic structure and source of meaning.

The wordy rites for ministry to the sick through most of the Prayer Book tradition had their genesis in a situation far removed from our own. First, serious illness in centuries past brought with it the possibility or even the likelihood of death, which is no longer necessarily the case. The sudden onset of serious heart disease, to cite but one example, might have portended death in the not-so-distant past. The sophisticated technologies, surgical procedures, and drug therapies required to treat this disease remind us that it is still serious and often life-threatening. Heart disease retains its position as the number one cause of death in western cultures, but it is treatable to the extent that it once was not, even a few decades ago. It does not invariably have to mean that death is imminent or likely. Medical technology thus has changed our attitudes toward

---

[4]Hatchett, *Commentary on the American Prayer Book*, 430; Wheatly, *Rational Illustration*, 10. 2.; and Marshall, *Prayer Book Parallels*, 1:438ff.

[5]See, for example, the communal responsibility implicit in the question put to the congregation by the celebrant, "Will all of you witnessing these promises do all in your power to uphold these two persons in their marriage?" BCP 1979, 425.

illness, even a serious one, simply because people are more likely to get well. At the same time, these life-extending therapies can be painful, lengthy, and isolating, and may hold terrors all of their own.

Second, in late medieval and reformation times a "good death" usually involved the opportunity for a final gathering of family *and community* at the deathbed. Thus sudden death was feared, for it deprived a person of the opportunity for that final experience of the community and its sacraments. Accordingly, the litany prayed for deliverance from "sudden death," an oddity to moderns who often voice a desire to "go quickly" perhaps to escape the pain af a lengthy death or the indignities brought with the miracles of modern medicine and life support.[6] Sickness and dying were thus communal events in medieval and reformation cultures.[7] In modern American culture, sickness and dying have become privatized, often cloistered away in a hospital room or in some other institution.

BCP 1979 wisely does not return to medieval or reformation models of ministering to the sick, for the sensibilities around illness have changed dramatically. But this Prayer Book does draw insights from the earlier sensibilities about community. BCP 1979, for example, does not impose a crowded communal setting on our cultural situation in which sickness and death have become more private moments. Modern medical therapies can exhaust sick per-

---

[6]Brightman, *English Rite*, 1:176–77. The Great Litany in BCP 1979 adapts this earlier sensibility to the contemporary situation, as it prays no longer for deliverance from "sudden death" but from "dying suddenly *and unprepared*." (Emphasis added.) Indeed, if the pastoral issue no longer resides in the fear of sudden death, the often unnamed issue of death not prepared-for remains. BCP 1928, 54; BCP 1979, 149.

[7]See the excellent historical treatment of these issues in Philippe Ariés, *The Hour of Our Death*, trans. Helen Weaver (New York: Alfred A. Knopf, 1982), 96–139.

sons, and a stream of visitors, much less a crowd, can intensify the exhaustion. And thus many hospitals put limits on visitors. There are rules, and reasonable ones, preventing the familiar scenes surrounding sickness in earlier times. But BCP 1979 does recover enough of the communal elements to balance what is often the excessive loneliness experienced by the sick and dying in American culture. The first rubric in the order for ministration to the sick differs little from that in Prayer Books from 1662 forward: "In case of illness, the Minister of the Congregation is to be notified."[8] Such notification is a *personal* responsibility that allows *communal* involvement.[9] That involvement might take its shape through prayer, support of the families, or actual visitation. The priest or deacon or layperson visiting the person who is ill carries along the symbols of the community—its scriptures, its ministry of healing, and its eucharistic sacrament.[10] Such ministry re-presents the concern of the larger community of faith, even when the cultural

---

[8]BCP 1979, 453.

[9]Wheatly, *Rational Illustration*, 10. 1. 1. Some communities might want to plan for an occasional corporate service for ministry to the sick, to emphasize the communal aspect of the church's ministrations. One possibility would be to note the Sunday lectionary for its attention to Jesus' ministry of healing and to plan such a service at the eucharist on one of those occasions. See "A Public Service for Healing," in *The Book of Occasional Services*, 166–73.

[10]These correspond to the three sections of the ministration: Part I: Ministry of the Word, Part II: Laying on of Hands and Anointing, and Part III: Holy Communion. The pertinent rubric reads: "At the Ministration, one or more parts of the . . . service are used, as appropriate; but when two or more are used together, they are used in the order indicated." BCP 1979, 453. A deacon or layperson always may lead Part I. If necessary, a deacon or layperson may do the anointing in Part II, using oil blessed by a bishop or priest. A deacon could carry communion from the reserved sacrament to the sick person but could not celebrate the eucharist. A deacon or duly licensed laypersons could carry communion directly from the altar at the chief celebration on Sundays. *The Book of Occasional Services*, 226–30.

situation does not make it desirable or possible for all or most of that community to be present.[11] Community thus provides a point of reference for this rite.[12]

Similarly, the "Reconciliation of a Penitent" looks to the community for the meaning of the rite, despite an essential private nature presented in this service. It is intended as a matter between priest and penitent and no one else, a "special confession"[13] taking into account the needs of those with troubled consciences. It is thus distinguished from the general confession at the daily office or the eucharist. Earlier Prayer Books provided for this special confession in the rubrics for the visitation of the sick, offering a form for absolution but not for the confession itself. BCP 1979 explicitly broadens the opportunities for confession, stating that the rite "is not restricted to times of sickness."[14] This Prayer Book is also the first to provide the penitent's part of the rite, not just the priest's form for absolution. Two forms for "private confession," as this rite is often called, are included. The private setting provides the pastoral opportunity for a penitent to name his or her sins specifically, hear the counsel of a pastor, and receive absolution. But the point of reconciliation is the recovery of community—specifically the community one enjoys with God, with

---

[11]The rubric for lay eucharistic ministers reads: "The Lay Eucharistic Minister should be accompanied by other persons from the congregation." And elsewhere: "It is desirable that other parishioners, relatives, and friends also be present to communicate with the person visited." *The Book of Occasional Services*, 227, 226.

[12]And a point of reference for the Ministration at the Time of Death, in which the rubric reads: "When possible, it is desirable that members of the family and friends come together to join in the Litany [at the Time of Death]." BCP 1979, 462.

[13]Brightman, *English Rite*, 2:828–29.

[14]BCP 1979, 446.

brothers and sisters, and, as the early church understood it, the community of the church itself. The church's ministry of reconciliation provides an antidote to the alienation caused by sin. The first rubric in the section "Concerning the Service" reads:

> The ministry of reconciliation, which has been committed by Christ to his Church, is exercised through the care each Christian has for others, through the common prayer of Christians assembled for public worship, and through the priesthood of the Church and its ministers declaring absolution.[15]

The ministry of reconciliation in its ritual form suggested in the Prayer Book can help a community to discover these other essentially communal ministries.[16] Planners need this broad perspective of the church's reconciling ministry. They will have little need to consider the dispatch of the rite, simple in its expectations with but two participants. Planners may, however, find themselves with opportunities to encourage the pastoral use of the rite in their parish, to ritualize and give a wider awareness of the church's reconciling work as that takes shape in their own community. The rich baptismal and communal imagery in the penitent's portion of form two might suggest some possibilities.[17]

"A Form of Commitment to Christian Service," new in BCP 1979, makes it possible for communities to acknowledge and support anyone who will undertake some new ministry or mission. The first rubric reads:

---

[15]Ibid.

[16]Interestingly, the Prayer Book also allows deacons and layfolk to hear confessions; it does not limit the ministry to priests and bishops. Deacons and layfolk engaged in this ministry may not, however, pronounce absolution. The Prayer Book provides a "declaration of forgiveness" instead.

[17]BCP 1979, 450. See Clark Hyde, *To Declare God's Forgiveness: Toward a Pastoral Theology of Reconciliation* (Wilton, CT: Morehouse-Barlow, 1984), especially 102–40, for the place of this rite in building a sense of community.

This form may be used when a person wishes to make or renew a commitment to the service of Christ in the world, either in general terms, or upon undertaking some special responsibility.[18]

The rubrics describe the various elements to include in the service, but they do not specify the form of commitment, a matter left to the planners. The provision of this communal rite allows individuals to celebrate the corporate aspect of a call to ministry, an oft-neglected aspect. The service might accordingly find appropriate use as a parish sees someone off to seminary. It might also be used to commission persons undertaking a brief medical mission abroad, or persons beginning a ministry with hospice or among the homeless, or persons exploring seriously the wide possibilities suggested in the ministry of a deacon. The service holds out the truth that whatever ministry a person undertakes, it represents the ministry of the *whole* church.

"A Thanksgiving for the Birth or Adoption of a Child" replaces the service for the "churching of women" from earlier Prayer Books.[19] That earlier service carried an interesting meaning for a woman's relationship with the community, for it derived from notions of ritual purity described in Leviticus 12. The crisis of birth put a woman in an ambiguous relationship with the worshiping community, leaving her "unclean" for the community's rites. So the various details in Leviticus describe when and by what rituals a woman could be made "clean" and return to her rightful place in the community. The churching of women follows this sensibility, describing a woman's re-entry into the community's worship following the trauma of birth. And prior to the advances of

---

[18]BCP 1979, 420.

[19]The complete name for the service, in every Prayer Book since 1552, has been "The Thanksgiving of Women after Child-birth, Commonly called the Churching of Women." Brightman, *English Rite*, 2:881–85; Marshall, *Prayer Book Parallels*, 1:462–73.

modern medicine, with antibiotics, monitoring procedures, and surgical techniques, every birth threatened death, both for mother and newborn. Thus every safe delivery marked the passage through an obviously dangerous time. The rite also drew on this understanding.

The birth of a child portends a change in life for most moderns in North American culture, and this life passage will usually result in the reordering of relationships with various communities, including the community of faith. But using the language of ritual purity to describe this reordering of relationships fits neither the experience nor the theological understanding of most people giving birth. Most women in childbirth, and the men who are their partners, would find it odd if not offensive and even misogynistic, to describe the birthing process as leaving mother and child "unclean" for anything. The trauma and joy of labor and giving birth are experienced as life-changing, but people today usually describe this passage as life-affirming, not as an event calling for the need of "purification."

The service in BCP 1979 takes into account these sensibilities and offers a life-affirming liturgy to mark the passage and new relationship. It ordinarily includes both parents, not just the mother. The first rubric reads:

> As soon as convenient after the birth of a child, or after receiving a child by adoption, the parents, with other members of the family, should come to the church to be welcomed by the congregation and to give thanks to Almighty God. It is desirable that this take place at a Sunday service. In the Eucharist it may follow the Prayers of the People preceding the Offertory. At Morning or Evening Prayer it may take place before the close of the Office.[20]

The Prayer Book intends that the community understand birth as an occasion to celebrate. Although the rubrics allow for the adap-

---

[20]BCP 1979, 439.

tation of the rite for use in the hospital or at home, its fullest meaning becomes obvious as the community gathers to worship.[21]

Planners can consider ways to implement this sensibility in ways to support parents of newborns and parents beginning an adoptive relationship. The ritual structures around this passage, together with the support of a community, can become crucial. In today's mobile society, people will often become parents in locales far away from their own mothers and fathers and other family, a fact inviting support from other quarters, including the church. Planners might even consider a communal liturgy, in the manner suggested by the rubrics, for every birth or adoption in the parish. Such a norm could provide a structure of support, and it could suggest several practical ministries to carry parents of newborns through this life passage—meals, babysitting, support groups, etc.[22] Moreover, planners in parishes who decide to defer baptisms to the five baptismal occasions suggested by the Prayer Book may find in this rite a helpful, even necessary, pastoral resource to recognize and celebrate birth or adoption. This norm could be more awkward to set in place in large parishes with births happening every week or two, and it might require some adaptation in these settings, for it is not desirable to overwhelm the weekly Sunday eucharist with this or any of the pastoral rites. Large parishes could still designate a Sunday every two or three months for the rite to maintain its place in the life of the community. Alternatively, a communal context could be sustained by planning to celebrate this rite at the daily office or at a weekday eucharist.

---

[21]Ibid.

[22]*The Book of Occasional Services* offers a more detailed structure for support through the crisis of pregnancy and childbirth as a parallel to the catechumenal process. See *The Book of Occasional Services*, 154–60.

Life's final crisis—and final conversion—comes in death, and the Prayer Book describes a communal liturgy to mark this passage. Privatized and death-denying notions about death and its rituals abound in North American culture. These cultural pressures may run counter to the communal understanding in the Prayer Book rites, where the first rubrics read:

> The death of a member of the Church should be reported as soon as possible to, and arrangements for the funeral should be made in consultation with, the Minister of the Congregation.

> Baptized Christians are properly buried from the church. The service should be held at a time when the congregation has opportunity to be present.[23]

The early Prayer Books assume the same communal sensibility, an assumption detailed by Wheatly. For example, he describes the importance of ringing the bell to call the community to the church for the burial rites.[24] And evening, he notes, was a usual time for

---

[23]BCP 1979, 468.

[24]Wheatly, *Rational Illustration*, 12. 2. The priest would meet the body and lead the procession "into the churche or towardes the graue." Brightman, *English Rite*, 2:848–49. The churchgrounds were almost invariably the only place for burial, and the early Prayer Books describe a rite *for the burying*. Many or most of those present would actually participate in the physical act of burying, mostly by helping fill in the grave. The office, if it had not already been said, would follow in the church. It was not unknown for the body to be brought to the church before burial (see Hatchett, *Commentary on the American Prayer Book*, 480 and Legg, *English Church Life*, 201), but the more common practice involved a direct procession to the grave. Wheatly interprets the rubric describing the procession "into the churche or towardes the graue" as naming the two likely places for burial, for indeed some were buried in the church (that is, either entombed in a sarcophagus or buried under the floors within the walls), although most were buried in the churchyard. Wheatly, *Rational Illustration*, 12.2.6. Moreover, burial soon after death was the norm, primarily for reasons of public health, but such an immediate burial also brought a first and undeniable step to begin the process of grieving. Perhaps the tolling of the bell would occasionally give the community

burial, rich with associations with the dead—the grave a resting place, death a kind of sleep.[25] But funerals in the evening would also make it possible for workers, otherwise occupied during daylight hours, to be present for the burial. The custom of late afternoon or evening burials supported the participation of the broader community.

BCP 1549 concluded the burial rites with a celebration of the eucharist, but subsequent Prayer Books deleted it.[26] BCP 1928 was the first book since BCP 1549 to provide eucharistic propers for use at burial but did not integrate the eucharist into the burial rite. BCP 1979 accomplishes this integration, structuring the materials for the burial office to serve as the liturgy of the word for the eucharist. And although the eucharist remains optional, certainly the intent for any liturgy of the resurrection rightly includes the community's eucharistic feast, a resurrection meal belonging to the celebration on the first day of each week, the day of resurrection.

---

its first notice of a death. But the point remains: the Prayer Book sensibility provided for the participation of a whole community affected by the death. And it assumed the burial would take place wherever the community worshiped, either in its church building or on the grounds surrounding the church.

[25]Wheatly, *Rational Illustration*, 12. 2. His describing the custom, however, does not mean that it was universal.

[26]L'Estrange includes the eucharist with his service and argues carefully for preserving this practice attested from the writings of the early church. Wheatly, quoting Cosin, also notes the propriety of celebrating the eucharist at burials and tacitly (but guardedly) countenances the practice. Sparrow, although writing more tersely, follows Wheatly on this point. Hatchett notes that at least occasionally the eucharist was celebrated at burials and, as with Edward VI, celebrated in the presence of the body. L'Estrange, *Alliance of Divine Offices*, 433–34, 457–62; Wheatly, *Rational Illustration*, 12.5.3.; Sparrow, *Rationale*, 59. 7.; and Hatchett, *Commentary on the American Prayer Book*, 480.

A Principle Inferred from the Tradition

I have devoted no little space to considering the various ways that the pastoral offices mark personal passages in life but do so with meaning for the entire community. Even on those occasions when the office must be private, as with reconciliation or in certain circumstances of ministration to the sick, the community remains a point of reference. I have made this point, I hope, without begging the question of its importance, for not only can this principle ease many anxieties faced by planners, but it can also bring clarity to any customary or set of guidelines that they might draft, especially for the most public of the pastoral rites, weddings and funerals.

The working principle is this: The community's pattern of worship on Sunday can describe a norm for all the pastoral offices. The application of the principle is simple, and it can clarify the expectations people bring to weddings and (to a lesser extent) to funerals. Such an approach can allow planners to state expectations for wedding music, for example, without having to resort to lists of "acceptable" and "not acceptable" pieces. Musicians and clergy, with the bride and groom, following this principle, could ask but two questions: Does our parish use the music under consideration during Sunday worship? If not, is it of the sort that *might* be used? This norm can also *encourage* certain kinds of music at weddings and funerals, particularly congregational hymn-singing, one of the usual Sunday norms. Bride and groom still might not like their having to exclude a favorite piece of popular music from the wedding, but at least with this approach the planners can explain the decision without having to make the explanation overly convoluted.

This working principle also allows flexibility, and it provides a usable guideline for addressing the unforeseen circumstances that arise fairly often in the pastoral rites. Moreover, it can describe a ceremonial style in line with the worshiping community and thus address those occasional tugs in the pastoral offices toward the eccentric or the grandiose. And if the eucharist is indeed the normal worship on Sundays, then the parish may decide on the eucharist as the norm (though not necessarily an absolute) for weddings and funerals. Planners can also decide to apply the usual ceremonial approach of the parish to these services, and they might even use this communal principle in addressing where the church's liturgies take place.

Urban T. Holmes begins with baptism to summarize what might be described as a communal sensibility for the pastoral offices:

> The Anglican pastoral ideal is one of care from birth to death. . . . When an individual is born he or she is brought to the church to be baptized in the presence of the congregation at Sunday worship. So-called private baptisms are a contradiction of the symbolism of the sacrament. When that same person seeks the solemnization of his or her marriage they come to the church to receive God's blessing and to witness with their spouse to their intention. There is no more fitting place to make this witness before God and his people. "Tying the knot" at home plate, on the beach, or while skiing downhill is not only tacky, it trivializes marriage. When we die it is only right that our fellow Christians grieve our departure by offering the Eucharist in the presence of our body in the church. Anglicans are not buried from commercial funeral chapels, if they understand the nature of their faith.[27]

Does this principle of a communal norm provide also for the necessary personal element? Yes, for the norms of worship in any community will be spacious enough to invite the principal participants into the planning—that is, giving then a say in the choices about music, lay ministers, readings, and the various options in the rite, etc. Let us recognize that communal norms do set limits, and some individuals will find any such limits stifling. Most pas-

---

[27]Holmes, *What Is Anglicanism?* 63.

tors, nonetheless, can enable the people involved to find a personal voice within the communal context. And usually that personal voice emerging from the communal will ring true, to the occasional surprise of skeptical individualists.

Finally, celebrants need to take seriously the place of the preached word, especially at weddings and funerals. Here a carefully crafted homily can bridge the story of persons to the larger story of community. Boilerplate homilies that avoid the personal story miss this connection. But maudlin or sentimental sermons, trivializing the personal or (worse) failing to speak truthfully, likewise miss the point. The preacher needs to honor both the points of reference, the personal and the communal. Making a truthful connection between the personal story and the story of scripture marks the preacher's challenge.

The Pastoral Offices and Ritual Clarity

The desire to make the pastoral offices meaningful and personal may lead some planners (particularly clergy) to try too hard. Extraneous and overly dramatic gestures may do more to obscure the meaning of the rite than to bring new meaning. Planners might ask: How much explanation does this gesture or that movement require? The crucial actions in the pastoral offices derive from the church's longer tradition, in which these basic actions are straightforward and require little if any explanation. The actions carry their own explanation—the joining of hands following the vows at a wedding, the laying on of hands or anointing at the ministration to the sick, the casting of dirt into a grave at a burial. However, the depth of significance in these actions makes them inexhaustibly meaningful, the base meaning of the Greek word *musterion*—mystery. The Christian mysteries are not esoteric. They require no secret knowledge. They do not obscure the meaning of the action itself or any of the surrounding actions. They do not leave people wondering if some gesture is *supposed* to mean something, and if so, what.

At a marriage, for example, the rubric following the exchange of vows requires the priest to join the right hands of the man and woman.[28] The vows, representing the heart of the marriage covenant, are essential, and the solemn joining of hands, with the pronouncement that follows, follows logically.[29] The most obvious gesture to signify the joining is for the priest to grasp and hold together the hands of the man and woman. Such an action requires little explanation. Wheatly writes, "The joining of hands naturally signifies contracting a friendship, and making a covenant . . . ."[30] But Kenneth Stevenson, in sketching the history of Anglican marriage rites and ceremonial, sarcastically describes a common bit of ceremony used at the joining of hands that became popular early in the twentieth century:

> We are now well into the era where Anglo-Catholics begin to do meaningful little ceremonies like tying stoles round couples' hands (which probably sent Cranmer into multiple rotations in his grave).[31]

---

[28]BCP 1979, 428.

[29]9An Order for Marriage, BCP 1979 435–36, provides in outline form an alternative rite for weddings. Like An Order for Celebrating the Holy Eucharist, this rite provides great flexibility. Parishes, if they choose to use it at all, might preserve it for the most extraordinary of circumstances. But even here, where flexibility is allowed and creativity encouraged, the vows are to be used as printed and without variation—as if to suggest that everything but the vows might be negotiable. Here is the crux of the marriage rite.

[30]Wheatly, *Rational Illustration*, 5. 2.

[31]Kenneth Stevenson, *Nuptial Blessing: A Study of Christian Marriage Rites*, Alcuin Club Studies, Number 64 (London: SPCK, 1982), 152. Stevenson's footnote details the absence of this custom in English usage until it was appropriated by twentieth-century anglo-catholics from a sixteenth-century French ceremony, by way of a later (and isolated) Italian rite!

Cranmer aside and more to the point, what does the wrapping of hands in a stole mean? This is a dramatic, although sometimes awkward, gesture, drawing attention to itself. Is it so dramatic that it draws attention from the arguably more important exchange of vows? Does it suggest an excessive clericalism, with the use of the priest's vesture of office for the joining of hands? Does it even suggest a depersonalization in the rite and its ceremonial, since the stole-wrapping makes it possible for the priest not to touch the couple at this point? I bring up this ceremonial detail, not to deride priests who in good faith have followed a popular convention at weddings, but to encourage the careful questioning of this and every aspect of ceremonial. What, if anything, does this gesture convey? Does it undermine or contradict other, perhaps more important meanings in the rite? Can it be explained? How complicated an explanation does it require? Again, the Anglican rule of simplicity provides an approach with the clearer and richer meaning. The more elaborate, esoteric gesture, intended to be more meaningful, ironically presents the possibility of obscured meaning—or even a wrong meaning.

The ministration to the sick includes an optional rite of anointing, an ancient usage with several layers of meaning. Olive oil was a basic medicine in the Mediterranean world. It could be a balm to rub on wounds or aching muscles or it could be taken internally. Often mixed with herbs or other medications, it could also be used by itself. Oil thus provided a medicine for use in many situations. But believers in Jesus also acclaimed him as the messiah (*mesuach* in Hebrew, *christos* in Greek), a word meaning, literally, "anointed one." Christians thus employing oil in their rites of healing first drew on its ordinary use as medicine.[32] But the meaning of anointing the sick did not end there for people who proclaimed faith in

---

[32]James 5:14; Mark 6:13.

Jesus the messiah. So the anointing became for them a way of celebrating the presence of Christ in the midst of sickness and a way of recalling his ministry of healing. Implicit in this use of oil was also the identification of the person being anointed with Jesus-the-anointed-one. The person anointed thus can become a sacramental person, revealing through the experience of sickness or infirmity something about the identity "in Christ," to use a familiar phrase from Paul's epistles. The person can actually enflesh —incarnate—this presence in Christ through the mystery of illness, reflecting on occasion the central mystery of Christ's suffering and death on the cross. In the unlikely circumstances of sickness, and in inexplicable ways, the presence of Jesus can be celebrated. The oil sacramentalizes the presence, and BCP 1979 allows, even encourages, its use.[33]

But who should be anointed? The church during the middle ages undoubtedly restricted its use too much, making anointing into a rite of dying—"extreme unction." Some contemporary uses of oil, however, may swing too far in the other direction. It is not uncommon, for example, for people to be anointed on behalf of someone else. But this usage, although popular in some circles, represents a basic misunderstanding of the sacrament. In the same way that no one would take penicillin on behalf of someone else (or be baptized on behalf of someone else), it is off the mark for one person to be anointed "for another." It is appropriate to pray for someone who is sick. It is not appropriate to take someone's

---

[33]BCP 1549 restored the anointing as a rite of healing. During the middle ages the rite had been so narrowly focused that it became a rite of dying, the "last rites." The first Prayer Book acknowledged its use at death but extended it to other, less extreme circumstances also. BCP 1552 dropped the anointing from the ministry to the sick, and subsequent Prayer Books followed this pattern. BCP 1928 provided the rubric to allow the option for anointing, but the full rite (including a presbyteral prayer for blessing the oil) did not come until BCP 1979.

medicine, sacramental or otherwise, even if that person will not or cannot take it for himself or herself.

How seriously ill does a person have to be for the anointing? Again, the criterion of the middle ages is too stringent. One does not have to be dying or even anywhere close to death for the oil to find appropriate use. But on the other hand, the rite should not be used in trivial or offhand ways. To anoint someone who is by all signs well is to misunderstand the origin and intent of the sacrament. There should be some identifiable, palpable infirmity—physical, emotional, mental or spiritual—or else the sacrament's innate meaning becomes obscured.[34]

A final example regarding ritual clarity comes in the burial rite. For most of Prayer Book history, the rite accompanied and interpreted the action of burying the dead. The Prayer Books assumed nothing other than that the body would be placed in the grave and that the grave would be filled in (or at least nearly so) during the rite itself, not afterward. BCP 1979 does nothing to move away from this assumption,[35] although North American funeral customs have undermined the practice. Ordinarily the committal ends with the casket still above ground, and this is the assumption of most funeral directors. Since this is what they have usually experienced at the cemetery, most churchpeople expect this as the norm. Might it not be better, however, to complete the burial during the rite? The experience of the burial and its power to confront the mourners with death's finality could move people

---

[34]See my article, "I Have Anointed My Servant: The Oils of the Prayer Book, Their Use and Meaning," *St. Luke's Journal of Theology* 24 (June 1991):49–63.

[35]The rubric reads, "Then, while earth is cast upon the coffin, the Celebrant says these words," after which comes an adaptation of the traditional Anglican text for committal. BCP 1979, 485, 501. This rubric changes nothing of substance from the earlier Prayer Books. Brightman, *English Rite*, 2:858–59; and Marshall, *Prayer Book Parallels*, 1:552–53.

more adequately through the process of grieving. The rites of burial surround this awe-inspiring action with the church's proc-lamation of death-and-resurrection, a supportive context of belief. An actual burying of the dead does not allow much room for denying death's reality. I recognize that the contemporary norms for burial mitigate against such a practice from the tradition. Many churchpeople and funeral directors will resist it. But it is the sort of issue that planners need the freedom to raise. And at very least priests can decide that the ritual casting of earth on the coffin deserves to come from the soil (too often discretely kept from view underneath a carpet of fake grass) that will fill in the grave. Priests can refuse the funeral director's vial of clean white sand or—worse still—a hand-full of petals. Even if the community cannot over-come the societal inertia that prevents them from actually burying their dead, at least the community's ministers can insist on main-taining a clearer sign of burial than suggested with flowers or antiseptic sand.

These three examples do not constitute an exhaustive list for issues of ritual clarity in the pastoral offices. But they do point out the need for identifying and understanding the central actions in a rite. These actions deserve emphasis in the liturgies. A clear, direct ceremonial can highlight the central actions, which convey their own meaning. Efforts to "make" the liturgies "meaningful," however, usually miss the mark. The central actions have their own meaning. Planners can find ways to trust that meaning. This principle can also help planners address some of the extraneities common to the pastoral offices—"unity" candles at marriages, excessive floral displays, photographers whose practices distract from or even take over the celebration, "eulogies" (sounding rather like canonization addresses) at funerals. It is helpful to know what is important—and what is not.

Preparation for the Pastoral Offices

Planners can expect that their discussions around the Pastoral Offices will eventually include questions about personal preparation. Canon law requires the clergy to take responsibility in preparing couples for marriage (and the blessing of a civil marriage) as well as candidates for confirmation.[36] The people anticipating these pastoral rites—and commitment to Christian service—deserve the chance to know what it is that they are getting into. They deserve the support of the community whose voice they take on as their own through the rite, and they deserve the opportunity to question that communal voice, if that is their need. The community also needs to understand the personal ambivalence that many people will bring to these communal rites and learn to be non-anxious in the face of that ambivalence. But on the other hand, the community deserves to state clearly what it expects from anyone preparing for one of the pastoral offices, for ultimately it is the community's voice in the rites. Who besides the clergy should be involved in the preparation? How long should it last? What issues should it include? Does the community expect candidates to be members of the parish—or alternatively, to worship with the parish for a certain period of time? Are the stated expectations definite criteria or are they more flexible guidelines? Each community can find its own peculiar voice in stating such expectations.

Often clergy will welcome or even insist on a parish's efforts in expressing its expectations, for confirmations, weddings, and even baptisms can become battlegrounds, with the clergy in the crossfire. Clergy may have one set of expectations, the parish another set (or various sets), and the surrounding culture another set altogether. When these expectations clash, clergy learn to expect

---

[36]Canon 1.18., 1.19., and 3.14.2(d).

turmoil. Clergy and parish can become aware of the turmoil and decide to work toward a consensus of understanding around their expectations. A parish's efforts to express heretofore unarticulated expectations can itself bear fruit for the relationship between priest and community. That is, this work can become one means of strengthening the pastoral relationship. The discipline of this work can also help a community recognize the tremendous opportunity presented in the pastoral offices with their interplay between the personal and communal. Attention to the details around these offices can enable a local community to discover more adequately its own ritual voice, not a different voice from that of the Prayer Book rites but one taking its own peculiar overtones from the larger tradition. A document describing a customary or parish guidelines is helpful, but the conversations leading up to the document are at least as important as the finished document. A parish that is attentive to these matters begins to learn something about the creative tension of the Anglican pastoral approach, the care and nurture of persons-in-community.

CHAPTER 6

Planning the Liturgy

LITURGICAL CHANGE ALMOST INVARIABLY INVITES opposition. Not every reform results in scattered outbreaks of rioting and revolt, as did BCP 1549, but changes in the way people worship can signal times of emotional upheaval. Anyone who takes responsibility for planning the liturgy learns something about this dynamic. The Devon Rebels who resisted the first Prayer Book protested in favor of the Latin mass and hurled nasty remarks at the new liturgy, a collection of "Christmas games," as they called it.[1] To opponents of reform, changing the liturgy may seem nothing less than a trivialization of the sacred into a game. But those favoring revision likewise can bring a tremendous emotional energy to their considerations of the issue, and they too are capable of taking shots at the opposition. Most of Richard Hooker's work in *Ecclesiastical Polity* calmly answered the puritan forces clamoring for more change than the English church could muster. The liturgy—and especially liturgical change—has this way of drawing out highly charged responses. For good or ill, these reactions are often exaggerated to the point of surprising those responsible for the changes in the first place. Who would expect a major church fight centering upon the placement of flags in the

---

[1]Peter Newman Brooks, *Cranmer in Context* (Minneapolis: Fortress Press, 1989), 48.

church—and whether to carry them in procession? Who would expect the turmoil and gossip accompanying the introduction of loaf bread (rather than wafers) for the eucharist? Who would expect the vestry to dig in their heels in opposing a modest set of baptismal guidelines presented by the worship committee—but with the rector taking most of the blame? These situations are not hypothetical. They are actual cases that have come to my attention, and they testify to the seemingly overstated concern that many people take in the liturgy and all its details.

But perhaps this concern is not overstated. Perhaps the sometimes explosive response to the most minute change in the liturgy is an instinctive, folk articulation of the principle *lex orandi lex credendi* described in Chapter One. Our acts of worship do represent our beliefs, and a shift in the conduct of worship may also signal a shift in ways of believing. The liturgy does make a difference to any worshiping community, and these exaggerated responses to liturgical change may indicate nothing more than an instinctive awareness of liturgy's importance. The liturgy especially makes a difference to Anglicans, who derive much of their identity and most of their theology from the manners of worship. Worship leaders might take advantage of this high regard for the liturgy and learn to think of their work in charting liturgical change as a catalyst in the life of the whole community. A catalyst injudiciously applied in a chemical reaction can result in unanticipated, even explosive consequences. But the sage use of the catalyst—that little bit of something that goes a long way—can effect a more desirable reaction. Without the catalyst, the reaction may never happen at all.

So it is with liturgical planning and especially liturgical change. A small change in the liturgy may open the possibility of change in other aspects of congregational life. Correspondingly, inordinate resistance to some small change in worship may indicate a more serious logjam elsewhere. These points of resistance and possibility offer important clues to the pastor who wants to "discern the spirit" of a congregation.

I emphasize the importance of congregational discernment, understanding that most of pastoral ministry, including the planning of worship, is situational. Sometimes the situation requires an assertive change with the desired effect of opening up the liturgy—and opening up congregational life. It is too naive to say the one can mechanically cause the other, but the forces required to reconfigure the liturgy may bring with them the reconfiguring of parish leadership and the relationships within the congregation. For example, a parish grown stagnant, with an entrenched, perhaps exclusionary circle of leaders, might be one situation in which to take an assertive tack. It would not be unusual in the situation of a stagnant parish to find a stagnant liturgy. A strategy to end the inertia in the liturgy, and to do so dramatically, could have ramifications in the rest of parish life. Opening the liturgy by making it dramatically more participatory (for example), more the work of the people it is intended to be, could signal or even help shake loose a corresponding shift in other parts of parish life. In taking such a course, the planners—especially the priest—need to brace themselves for resistance, retaliation, and threats to leave the parish. They should expect such a response as part of the process, and thus they need a good dose of resolve before undertaking the work involved in such an abrupt but calculated change. Sometimes planning the liturgy (and ministering in a parish) will require this style of leadership.[2]

On the other hand some situations will require a more measured response, one that undertakes change only in the most

---

[2]See Roy M. Oswald, *Power Analysis of a Congregation* (Washington, DC: The Alban Institute, 1977) for a more detailed guide to various leadership styles.

moderate of fashions. A parish with a disabled leadership and demoralized membership, for example, might collapse under the pressures of any assertive change in the liturgy. In such a parish the priest and other planners might want to practice a careful, consultative style of leadership, drawing insights and opinions from every quarter—and only then move tentatively toward change. This approach could help the parish leadership discover (or rediscover) their power and take appropriate responsibility for the life of the community. It could also give the whole community a sense of stability and a sense of being taken seriously. A parish recovering from an excessively authoritarian or abusive leadership (often from a previous priest) or from some specific trauma in its life might require such a slow, measured pace of change.

The principle of situational leadership might seem obvious, but the existence of two rigid (and contradictory) schools of "conventional wisdom" suggest otherwise. The first piece of wisdom (so-called) would have every priest beginning a new ministry to "change everything you want to during the first six months, because this period will bring your best chance or maybe even your only chance for any change at all." This approach, often stated in uncompromising terms, errs in two regards. First, it leads the priest to assume that making changes in the liturgy or any place else is solely his or her prerogative and perhaps even a matter of personal taste or whim, as described in Chapter One. But the liturgy always remains the work of the whole people. The priest plays a pivotal role in organizing and leading this work, but it is not the role of the priest to play the arbitrary ruler. Yes, the euphoria of the first few months in a new ministry presents an opening for change, but often the changes that happen during that period take place apart from the priest's necessary work of discerning who the community is and what the community really needs. How could he or she have had the time for such discernment? And it also happens apart from the equally necessary work of convincing people about the meaning and importance of change, with a resulting lack of depth and endurance to the change.[3]

Second, this conventional wisdom errs in its assumption that the best chance for change comes early in a ministry. The more unshakable changes are likely to come later, after the priest has taken time to earn the trust of the community and has begun to learn his or her way around the relationships there. A renewed emphasis on longer tenures of ministry argues that five years or so into the work begins a new level of intimacy and possibility for the priest working with the people.[4]

The second approach, often stated in equally incontestable terms, would have the priest to make no change whatsoever during the early period of a new ministry.[5] If a priest were to choose between these two prevailing schools of conventional wisdom, this would be the obvious choice, for it is less likely to wreak havoc for priest or community. As a general principle, it has its place. As an absolute rule, however, it fails. Unfortunately, it is often taught as just such a rule. The fallacy in this approach is that it does not allow for situations that require change, and such situations may arise even during the first few months of ministry. Different situations call for different approaches, and such a cautious approach as this may blind priests and other leaders to the necessity of the moment. Moreover, this dictum may set the norm for a priest undervaluing his or her own authority in leading and organizing

---

[3]See Roy M. Oswald, *The Pastor as Newcomer* (Washington, DC: The Ablan Institute, 1977), 7–8.

[4]See, for example, Daniel V. Biles, *Pursuing Excellence in Ministry* (Washington, DC: Alban Institute, 1988), 79.

[5]At least six months, according to consultant Roy M. Oswald, in his influential and widely read work, *New Beginnings: Pastorate Start Up Workbook* (Washington, DC: The Alban Institute, 1977), 63–64.

the worship in a parish. The priest must always gauge the sense of the parish, but a priest overly concerned with watching his or her flank will become timid, unable to take the necessary risks in providing inspirited leadership.

Byron Stuhlman describes a middle way, one honoring the place of both priest and congregation:

> Celebrants should respect the liturgical style of the parishes in which they conduct worship. To fail to take into account a parish's preference for evangelical simplicity or for catholic ceremonial or to ignore the ethnic roots and traditions of a significant number of parishioners is to fail to relate to people as they really are. Presbyters may seek to move their parish from the periphery of Anglican liturgical or theological tradition toward the center or to broaden a narrow cultural or ethnic base, but they need to be sensitive to the traditions of the parish as they do so. . . .
>
> If clergy need to respect the integrity of a parish's tradition, so parishes need to respect the theological and liturgical integrity of one who presides at their worship. Celebrants should conform to the style of the parish insofar as possible, but should not be asked to do violence to their conscience in the process. Clergy and parishes both need to learn to *adapt to each other* in this matter.[6]

In the best of circumstances, liturgical planning that results in change will require the cunning of serpents and the innocence of doves.[7] Clergy and other planners will do well to equip themselves for this difficult but rewarding task. Some of the best material for this preparation comes from the discipline of family systems theory, out of which Edwin Friedman has written his now-familiar work entitled *Generation to Generation*.[8]

Friedman's holistic approach to congregational life as a *system* can help worship planners understand the dynamics of change

---

[6]Byron D. Stuhlman, *Prayer Book Rubrics Expanded* (New York: Church Hymnal Corporation, 1987), 209–11. Emphasis added.

[7]Matthew 10:16.

[8]Edwin H. Friedman, *Generation to Generation: Family Process in Church and Synagogue* (New York: The Guilford Press, 1985).

and the sometimes inordinate resistance to it. He invites his readers to leave behind simplistic notions about cause and effect: "If I can push hard enough, then I can force a change." Friedman counsels that pushing hard might be counterproductive. If I push hard to counter resistance, then the truth is that the resistance may push back, harder than before! Thus Friedman urges less pushing and more "playfulness" in seeking a way toward renewal in relationships and in systems. Appropriate humor, the use of paradox, and the leader's ability to "differentiate" from the larger system offer some key resources to effecting change. Friedman also writes that there are nodes in a system where savvy leaders might find a likely entry to effect change throughout, a fulcrum against which a little leverage might cause an otherwise intransigent object to begin moving. My contention is that the liturgy provides one such likely place in many congregations.

Having said all this, I must also warn against a manipulative and simple-minded tinkering with the liturgy, the sort of gimickry that undermines the dignity of Anglican worship. Not only does such tinkering debase the worship life of a community, but it is usually too transparent to work very well. Planners looking toward the liturgy as a place to effect change do well to work with a light touch and to beware of letting their agenda take over the parish's worship. Planners might need to know, for example, about serious conflict in the parish—not so they might contrive to use the liturgy as a "quick fix" for the conflict, but so they might have important information as a background for their work. With careful use of the knowledge they could at least avoid unintentionally awkward moments in the liturgy and manage not to make matters worse.

Planners do need to know what is going on in the life of the parish for reasons of both pastoral and strategic concern. Their primary purpose, however, remains nothing other than arranging the services of word and sacrament, even (perhaps especially) in the middle of conflict. They should avoid any impulse to use the liturgy as a means to "fix" the conflict. In these circumstances, many a priest or worship committee has resorted to planning a "service of healing" or "service of reconciliation," with the agenda of setting aright all those broken relationships. Clergy are often surprised at the palpable emptiness in such services; or they are surprised when no one "comes forward" for the healing. Pushing hard may result in people pushing back, even when the pushing comes in the liturgy. When I talk about finding in the liturgy a catalyst for change in the larger life of the parish, I have in mind nothing other than the careful planning of word and sacrament for the worshiping community. The necessary changes brought in this planning, incremental or sudden, according to the circumstances, will in their course signal changes or even bring them about in the larger community. That larger systemic change will ordinarily be gradual, appreciated over the long haul. Instantaneous change in the system is unlikely and should be suspect. And perhaps any instantaneous change should lead planners to examine their work for hidden agenda. My point is that savvy planners need an awareness that their work with the liturgy can effect change in the larger system and that they can even bring some intentionality to their work. They need an awareness of all the ramifications and possibilities of this fact. But they should never become Machiavellian in their processes.

The Place of the Rector

The final authority for planning the liturgy lies in the ministry of the rector, as the canons of the Episcopal Church state:

> The authority of and responsibility for the conduct of the worship and the spiritual jurisdiction of the Parish are vested in the Rector, subject to the

Rubrics of the Book of Common Prayer, the Constitution and Canons of the Church, and the pastoral direction of the Bishop.[9]

This canon stands first in the section entitled "Of Clergy and Their Duties," suggesting its preeminence in the ministry of a priest. Part of the priest's continuing vocational development involves an acceptance of this authority and responsibility. Some clergy, preferring to avoid conflict and recognizing the high demands placed on worship planners, simply try to dodge this obligation. Sometimes clergy react only when absolutely necessary. They develop patterns of passivity and avoidance when it comes to the liturgy; they might acquiesce or decide by not deciding. Other clergy, proactive rather than reactive in their approach, will still choose to yield entirely to the lay planners. These clergy may have high-minded ideals about enabling the laity, but whenever they remove themselves from the process of planning, they abdicate a crucial role invested in them through ordination.[10] The clergy can support lay planners best by accepting an appropriate (not authoritarian) role in taking final authority and responsibility for the liturgy. It is expected that the rector of a parish will have some training and expertise in the liturgy, a sufficient familiarity with liturgical issues to make credible his or her leadership among intelligent laypeople, most of whom will lack technical training on the subject. But it is not just that a priest has the proper education for this role in planning the liturgy; ordination by its nature sets a person apart for it. Through ordination the church invests its clergy with distinct responsibilities for the life of the entire community, including its life of worship. The clergy stand or fall with the appropriate ownership of these and similar responsibilities. A rector thus may choose to delegate certain aspects of this authority

---

[9]Canon 3. 14. 1(a).
[10]BCP 1979, 531–32.

or share it with others, but he or she may never choose to abdicate any of the responsibility for it. Healthy, full-blown lay leadership depends on a healthy, appropriately articulated ordained leadership.

A word about the worship canon cited above: The more a rector quotes the canon to settle an argument, the more he or she diminishes any personal authority on the issues of worship. Rectors should know their responsibilities and develop some sense of ease with them. Planning groups, musicians, other clergy in the parish, and worship committees need to know that they function as a council of advice to the rector. And they need to know the limits of their counsel. But the rector who finds it necessary to remind other planners of these relative roles ("I'm the rector and you're not") ironically betrays an uneasiness with appropriate authority. That authoritarian appeal to an extrinsic source of authority—the canons—will undermine the quality of personal and more authentic leadership that a rector has to offer. That leadership needs to be shaped by an acceptance of such roles as described in the canons. But no priest bolsters his or her standing by quoting the canon on worship. I know three priests who each lamented a continuing need (or felt need, at least) to remind a vestry or worship committee what the canons say about who is in charge of worship. In each case, this pattern turned out to be a first signal of serious conflict between priest and congregation. And in each case, the pastoral relationship ended in unhappy circumstances within six months' time; the priest was forced to leave.

Even so, a rector needs to find some way to assert a proper authority, and that challenge describes a large part of the pastoral ministry these days. Before the liturgical renewal of this century, the priest's task in arranging the liturgy was important but often mundane, as the literature suggests. He would study the Prayer Book, read Hooker's *Ecclesiastical Polity* (especially Book 5), or perhaps Sparrow or Wheatly or, if his sentiments were high church, L'Estrange. These works, however, did not address issues of pastoral liturgy as we now understand it. Hooker and Sparrow and all the rest defended the Prayer Book heritage and legitimacy, and they described *for the priest* how to use the Anglican liturgy. Some of these classical writings suggested resources for the priest to use in enriching the liturgy. L'Estrange falls into this category, as do the writings in the tractarian heritage. Although these writers from the classical period understood and described a communal ambiance of the liturgy, they assumed that the priest would take sole responsibility for it. Consulting with the laity to plan the liturgy would have been an idea alien to their consciousness. The laity did not lack in dignity, in the estimation of these writers, but the responsibilities of the laity were elsewhere. Priests were ordained for the liturgy, and many of them took the task of preparing for it with high seriousness.[11] But they did not ask the laity for insights to shape the planning, and the laity did not expect to be asked.

The liturgical movement of this century came as part of a sea change experienced by the church and all its ministers. The role of the *people* received a renewed emphasis, and the teaching about liturgy (and ministry in general) began to take into account the people's insights and their ministry. Theological schools could no longer teach liturgy as priest-craft informed by a legitimate Anglican heritage; they had to teach it as a work of the people in which the priest has a crucial part. And for the first time, especially with the wave of new liturgies in the 1960s and 1970s, the schools had to teach the art of implementation. Now it is assumed that priests will work with a worship committee (in larger parishes) or an informal planning group (in smaller parishes) as an ordinary part of their

---

[11]See Addleshaw, *Architectural Setting*, 73.

work around the liturgy. This no doubt leaves the priest's position more tenable, for he or she must stand between two, sometimes opposing forces, and remain accountable to both. On the one hand, the priest must answer to the Prayer Book tradition, as the canon states. On the other hand, he or she must answer to the people who call the liturgy their own work. Leaning too far in the one direction leaves the priest pedantic and authoritarian. Leaning too far the other way signals a willingness to surrender the tradition in favor of constant survey-taking. As is so often the case in the Anglican heritage, here again a middle way, as difficult as it may be, marks the place. Finding an appropriate authority in a comprehensive accountability to both tradition and people describes an important piece of ordained ministry.

The Place of a Worship Committee

Most priests these days will want to fulfill the canonical charge quoted above by taking counsel with representative laity of the parish. It makes good sense for everyone concerned. And it makes good sense for the liturgy. Worship committees provide one way for a priest to remain accountable to the people of the parish. But who should be on the committee, and how should the committee operate? There are several general issues to take into account before deciding.[12]

First is the purpose of the committee. Certainly the committee's primary purpose is to advise the rector, who must make the final decisions about the liturgy. But do the rector and parish look to the committee primarily for *representation* or for *leadership*? These are not mutually exclusive categories, but discerning an emphasis

---

[12]The pamphlet from the Associated Parishes, *The Parish Worship Committee* (Alexandria, VA: Associated Parishes, Inc., 1988) provides a good resource for worship planners. I make no effort to duplicate the fine work it presents.

could help shape the committee's membership. If the priest and people expect a pattern of stability, with slow, incremental change, then a representative committee would suit these purposes. Those responsible for forming a committee with an eye toward representation should take care to include all the diverse viewpoints and constituencies from the parish. The rector's primary work with such a committee, then, would lie in listening and establishing trust—not necessarily in acting on everything that comes up. With diverse constituencies and a desire for stability, a stated norm of consensus would be in order. Such a norm would allow no change in the liturgy until everyone in the working group—including the rector—can come to essential agreement on the issue. Equally important in such a working procedure is an agreement to support any actions taken. These two important components of working by consensus will assure that everyone gets a hearing and that change will occur slowly. There are pastoral circumstances that demand procedures just like these.

If, however, the priest and parish have in mind a renewed vision for the shape of the liturgy, then another tack might be in order. Those choosing the people to serve on the committee could take steps to include members committed to that vision. In some cases this might be the most important criterion for membership. The committee would then take its primary task not in *representing constituencies* but in *leading the parish* into new liturgical patterns. When dramatic changes are in order, this approach to committee formation is appropriate. People effective as communicators and educators make good choices in this approach, as do strong personalities.

Again, these two approaches to constituting the committee are not mutually exclusive. It does help, however, to state clearly any expectations for the work of the committee. Conflict is sure to happen if the rector expects strong and cooperative *leadership* from the committee while the various members assume that their most important task is to *lobby the rector* with the opinions from a guild, the early service, or the prayer-and-praise group.

This leads to a second set of issues to consider, the place of opinions in the work of the committee. Opinions are absolutely in order, or else committee meetings would result in a strange silence. But it is not unreasonable to expect that members learn to scrutinize their opinions from the perspective of the larger tradition. It is not unreasonable to expect that committee members know the rudiments of the Prayer Book or that they read a short list of books to provide a basic familiarity with the liturgical tradition. In many instances those choosing the members for the worship committee will want to make a basic familiarity with the tradition, or a willingness to obtain it, a criterion for serving. Sometimes an important piece of the committee's work, at least early on, will lie in their gaining the knowledge necessary to make informed recommendations to the rector. Opinions will always come to the committee, but it is not unreasonable to insist that these be *informed* opinions.

The educational functions of the committee, in fact, may be some of their most important. Much of their energies may be spent in educating themselves and in finding ways to communicate their learnings to the larger parish. Their commitment as a learning community can catalyze learning throughout the rest of the congregation. Diocesan seminars and workshops are often available, and committee members will want to avail themselves of these opportunities. In addition to this book, there is a short list of works on the liturgy that committee members could be expected to choose from. Such a list includes, among others: Howard Galley's *The Ceremonies of the Eucharist*[13]; Charles Price and Louis

---

[13]Howard Galley, *The Ceremonies of the Eucharist: A Guide to Celebration*

Weil's *Liturgy for Living*[14]; Byron D. Stuhlman's *Prayer Book Rubrics Expanded*; from the Roman Catholic idiom of worship, two books stand out for use by a worship committee, Robert Hovda's *Strong, Loving and Wise*[15]; and Aidan Kavanagh's *Elements of Rite*[16]. Committee members should have more than a passing knowledge of *The Hymnal 1982* and the Prayer Book, with special attention to rubrics and the various sections entitled "Concerning the Service." It is not necessary for the sake of their work that committee members become scholars or even quasi-seminary students. It is necessary, however, that they become informed learners, and committee members will do well to devote meeting time to discussing books and learning together, for the sake of the larger community they serve.

Who gets to name the members to serve on the committee? This question defines a third set of issues. The least desirable means of forming the committee is the "sign-up" method. If a person has enough interest to volunteer, then under this common method of selection he or she is included. This approach has the disadvantage of attracting people with axes to grind, and often their narrow agendas will stymie the work of the whole committee. Nonetheless, clergy will often find such a process in place as they begin a new ministry. It does not present an impossible situation, but it leaves little room for proactive selection of appropriate people for the work.

It is not unthinkable that the rector select the committee, since

(Cambridge, MA: Cowley Publications, 1989).

[14]Charles P. Price and Louis Weil, *Liturgy for Living*, *The Church's Teaching Series*, Volume 5 (San Francisco: Harper San Francisco, 1984).

[15]Robert Hovda, *Strong, Loving and Wise: Presiding in Liturgy* (Collegeville, MN: The Liturgical Press, 1983).

[16]Aidan Kavanagh, *Elements of Rite: A Handbook of Liturgical Style* (Collegeville, MN: The Liturgical Press, 1982).

he or she deserves to have some level of comfort in working with the people on the committee. It is, after all, an *advisory* group. The rector might also be in a position to know who might serve well. His or her input becomes all the more important if the leadership model describes the committee's primary direction. But building some means of accountability into such a selection process would be wise. Perhaps the rector could consult with the vestry before making the selections. Perhaps he or she could submit a number of nominees from which the vestry could choose. The rector can find some means of taking primary responsibility for forming the committee without taking unilateral (or even dictatorial) action.

But it is not unreasonable for someone other than the rector to take the lead in setting the committee, especially if the representative model gives a general direction for the work. Constituency groups in some circumstances could themselves ask a particular representative person to serve, so lectors, musicians, choir, altar guild, early service, and the vestry itself, might have a voice. No matter who does the choosing, it is not a bad idea to include people from the groups, like choir and lectors, directly involved in liturgical leadership. And the parish musician should *always* be included, for he or she brings particular and necessary expertise to the committee's work.

In some situations the vestry might be the appropriate body to take the lead in selecting the committee. The point is that different circumstances require different approaches, and no single approach will work in every situation.

A fourth set of issues pertains to the committee's life. How often should the committee meet? Do they meet regularly? Monthly? Seasonally? Or do they meet only when an issue arises?

Who presides at the meeting? Does the rector? Or does another designated chairperson? If the latter, who chooses—rector, vestry, or the committee itself? Is it automatically a vestry representative?

How long does the term of membership last? One year? Longer? Are there staggered multi-year terms? (In general it is desirable to provide for continuity without lapsing into the assumption that some people deserve permanent membership on the committee.)

Does the committee report its work to the vestry and the parish at large? Or does it communicate its recommendations only to the rector?

How much weight does the committee's recommendation carry with the rector? Is the recommendation the final word—or almost final? How much leeway does the committee (and vestry and parish) give the rector in accepting or rejecting the advice offered?

The priests I know generally fall into one of two groups as they tell of their experience with worship committees. One group tells horror stories, how the worship committee is the single most difficult and demanding bunch of people they have to work with. The meetings bring a regular occasion for conflict and are cause for dread. My sense of these embattled clergy is that they have done little to work through the issues named in this section and even less to provide the leadership necessary for the committee to know the parameters of its work.

The second group of clergy tell a different story altogether. For them the work with a worship committee is energizing and profitable, an opportunity to accomplish some good things for the life of the entire parish. And they draw genuinely helpful insights from the group. My sense of these clergy is that they did not just happen on a good committee by chance. Instead, their own knowledge of the liturgy, their pastoral attention to issues like those described in this section, and the leadership they bring to the deliberations of the committee all work to their advantage—and the parish's. I do not mean that their experience is conflict-free. But with the savvy of serpents and the innocence of doves, they weather the conflict and even benefit from it. Their work in planning worship provides a catalyst for conversion of life far beyond the confines of the liturgy proper.

A Final Note

A penchant for revision describes one piece of the Anglican liturgical ethos. No one can assume that the Prayer Book we have will never change. If we understand the tradition, we should assume that there will be revisions and more revisions in the way we worship.

Planners do well to take this attitude to the liturgy in the parish. No one should assume that the way things are done now will remain appropriate for all time. A continuing discipline of evaluating will help planners shape the liturgy. Ceaseless tinkering takes the all-important familiarity out of the liturgy. But leaders can take a hard look at the liturgy without rearranging the furniture all the time. Does this idea, this movement, this gesture, this hymn, work or not? How might it work better? Planners can set aside periods of trial usage to test a new idea. But they should always evaluate in the aftermath, or else the trial period results in time wasted. Experiencing the liturgy and reflecting on it carefully can describe the continuing work of worship planners, even when no change is in sight.

Change-within-stability might well describe the Anglican attitude toward liturgical reform. On the one hand lies an abiding respect for tradition, a source of stability and, yes, pride. On the other hand lies an Anglican penchant for sanctification, a desire for growth in the Spirit, a theological bent toward perfectionism that tells us that we have not yet arrived, with more to learn and turns to make in our journeying.

Bibliography

Addleshaw, G. W. O. *The Architectural Setting of Anglican Worship: An Inquiry into the Arrangements for Public Worship in the Church of England from the Reformation to the Present Day*. London: Faber and Faber, 1948.

Ancient Christian Writers: The Works of the Fathers in Translation. Edited by Johannes Quasten and Joseph C. Plumpe. Vol. 6. Translated by James A. Kleist. Westminster, MD: Newman Press, 1948.

The Anglican Chant Psalter. Edited by Alec Wyton. New York: Church Hymnal Corporation, 1987.

The Anglican Missal. London: The Society of Ss. Peter and Paul, 1921.

Anglicanism: The Thought and Practice of the Church of England, Illustrated from the Religious Literature of the Seventeenth Century. Edited by Paul E. More and Frank L. Cross. London: SPCK, 1962.

Annotated Constitutions and Canons for the Government of the Protestant Episcopal Church in the United States of America, Otherwise Known as the Episcopal Church. 2 vols. New York: The Office of General Convention, 1985.

Ariés, Philippe. *The Hour of Our Death*. Translated by Helen Weaver. New York: Alfred A. Knopf, 1982.

Avis, Paul. *Anglicanism and the Christian Church: Theological Resources in Historical Perspective*. Minneapolis: Fortress Press, 1989.

The Baptismal Mystery and the Catechumenate. Edited by Michael Merriman. New York: Church Hymnal Corporation, 1990.

Biles, Daniel V. *Pursuing Excellence in Ministry*. Washington, DC: The Alban Institute, 1988.

The Book of Occasional Services: 1994. New York: Church Hymnal Corporation, 1995.

Brightman, F. E., ed. *The English Rite: Being a Synopsis of the Sources and Revisions of the Book of Common Prayer*. 2 vols. London: Rivingtons, 1915.

Brooks, Peter Newman. *Cranmer in Context*. Minneapolis: Fortress Press, 1989.

The Catechumenal Process: Adult Initiation and Formation for Christian Life and Ministry. Edited by Anne E. P. McElligott. New York: Church Hymnal Corporation, 1990.

Chambers, John David. *Divine Worship in England in the Thirteenth and Fourteenth Centuries Contrasted with and Adapted to that in the Nineteenth*. Rev. ed. London: Basil Montagu Pickering, 1877.

Crockett, William R. *Eucharist: Symbol of Transformation*. New York: Pueblo, 1989.

Davies, Horton. *Worship and Theology in England*. 5 vols. Princeton, NJ: Princeton University Press, 1965.

Dearmer, Percy. *The Parson's Handbook*. 12th ed. London: Oxford University Press, 1932; 1st ed., 1899.

Diocese of Milwaukee, "Living Our Baptismal Covenant: Diocese of Milwaukee." New York: Episcopal Church Center, 1989.

Dix, Gregory. *The Shape of the Liturgy*. London: Dacre Press, 1945.

The First and Second Prayer Books of Edward VI. New York: Everyman's Library, 1910, 1964.

Friedman, Edwin H. *Generation to Generation: Family Process in Church and Synagogue*. New York: The Guilford Press, 1985.

Galley, Howard. *The Ceremonies of the Eucharist: A Guide to Celebration*. Cambridge. MA: Cowley Publications, 1989.

Gore, Charles, ed. *Lux Mundi: A Series of Studies in the Religion of the Incarnation*. London: John Murray, 1889.

Hatchett, Marion J. *Commentary on the American Prayer Book*. New York: Seabury, 1981.

Hauerwas, Stanley, and Willimon, William H. *Resident Aliens: Life in the Christian Colony*. Nashville: Abingdon Press, 1989.

Hebert, A. G., ed. *The Parish Communion*. London: SPCK, 1937.

Hippolytus: A Text for Students. Translated by Geoffrey J. Cuming. Bramcote, England: Grove Booklets, 1976.

Holmes, Urban T. *What Is Anglicanism?* Wilton, CT: Morehouse-Barlow, 1982.

Hooker, Richard. *Of the Laws of Ecclesiastical Polity*. Vol. 1 and 2. *Everyman's Library*. New York: E. P. Dutton, 1907.

Hovda, Robert. *Strong, Loving and Wise: Presiding in the Liturgy*. Collegeville, MN: The Liturgical Press, 1983.

Hyde, Clark. *To Declare God's Forgiveness: Toward a Pastoral Theology of Reconciliation*. Wilton, CT: Morehouse-Barlow, 1984.

The Hymnal 1982, Accompaniment Edition. 2 vols. New York: Church Hymnal Corporation, 1985.

The Hymnal 1982 Companion. 4 vols. Edited by Raymond F. Glover. New York: Church Hymnal Corporation, 1990.

Iremonger, F. A. *William Temple, Archbishop of Canterbury: His Life and Letters.* London: Oxford University Press, 1948.

Kavanagh, Aidan. *Elements of Rite: A Handbook of Liturgical Style.* New York: Pueblo, 1982.

Legg, J. Wickham. *English Church Life from the Restoration to the Tractarian Movement.* London: Longmans, Green and Co., 1914.

Lesser Feasts and Fasts: 1994. New York: Church Hymnal Corporation, 1995.

L'Estrange, Hamon. *The Alliance of Divine Offices.* 4th ed. Oxford: John Henry Parker, 1846; 1st ed., 1690.

Marshall, Paul V. *Prayer Book Parallels.* 2 vols. New York: Church Hymnal Corporation, 1989, 1990.

Maurice, F. D. *The Kingdom of Christ or Hints to a Quaker Respecting the Principles, Constitution and Ordinances of the Catholic Church.* 2 vols. 2d ed. London: SCM, 1958; 2d ed. first published 1842; 1st ed., 1838.

Michno, Dennis G. *A Priest's Handbook: The Ceremonies of the Church.* Wilton, CT: Morehouse-Barlow, 1983.

The Occasional Papers of the Standing Liturgical Commission. Collection Number 1. New York: Church Hymnal Corporation, 1987.

Oswald, Roy M. *The Pastor as Newcomer.* Washington, DC: The Alban Institute, 1977.

———. *New Beginnings: Pastorate Start Up Workbook.* Washington, DC: The Alban Institute, 1977.

———. *Power Analysis of a Congregation.* Washington, DC: The Alban Institute, 1977.

The Parish Worship Committee. Alexandria, VA: Associated Parishes, Inc., 1988.

Parker, Andrew D. *Keeping the Promise: A Mentoring Program for Confirmation in the Episcopal Church.* Harrisburg, PA: Morehouse Publishing, 1994.

Pelikan, Jaroslav. *The Emergence of the Catholic Tradition.* Vol. 1, *The Christian Tradition: A History of the Development of Doctrine.* Chicago: University of Chicago Press, 1971.

The Plainsong Psalter. Edited by James Litton. New York: Church Hymnal Corporation, 1988.

Plater, Ormonde. *Intercession: A Theological and Practical Guide.* Cambridge, MA: Cowley Publications, 1995.

Prayers of the Eucharist: Early and Reformed. Edited by R. C. D. Jasper and G. J. Cuming. 2d ed. New York: Oxford University Press, 1980.

Price, Charles P., and Weil, Louis. *Liturgy for Living.* The Church's Teaching Series, Vol. 5. San Francisco: Harper San Francisco, 1994.

The Psalter Hymnal. Grand Rapids, MI: Eerdmans, 1987.

Pusey, E. B. *The Real Presence of the Body and Blood of Our Lord Jesus Christ: The Doctrine of the English Church.* Oxford: James Parker, 1869.

———. *Scriptural Views of Holy Baptism: As Established by the Consent of the Ancient Church, and Contrasted with the Systems of Modern Schools.* Oxford: J. H. Parker, 1836.

Ritual Notes on the Order of Divine Service. 5th ed. London: William Walker, 1907.

St. Benedict's Rule for Monasteries. Translated by Leonard J. Doyle. Collegeville, MN: The Liturgical Press, 1948.

Smith, George Wayne. "I Have Anointed My Servant: The Oils of the Prayer Book, Their Use and Meaning." *St. Luke's Journal of Theology* 24 (June 1991): 49-63.

Sparrow, Anthony. *A Rationale, or Practical Exposition of the Book of Common Prayer.* London: Charles Rivington, 1722; 1st ed., 1657.

Stevenson, Kenneth. *Nuptial Blessing: A Study of Christian Marriage Rites.* Alcuin Club Studies, Number 64. London: SPCK, 1982.

Stuhlman, Byron D. *Prayer Book Rubrics Expanded.* New York: Church Hymnal Corporation, 1987.

———. *Redeeming the Time: An Historical and Theological Study of the Church's Rule of Prayer and the Regular Services of the Church.* New York: Church Hymnal Corporation, 1992.

Supplemental Liturgical Materials. New York: Church Hymnal Corporation, 1991.

Taft, Robert. *The Liturgy of the Hours in East and West: The Origins of the Divine Office and Its Meaning for Today.* Collegeville, MN: The Liturgical Press, 1986.

Talley, Thomas J. *The Origins of the Liturgical Year.* New York: Pueblo, 1986.

Thornton, Martin. *English Spirituality: An Outline of Ascetical Theology According to the English Pastoral Tradition.* London: SPCK, 1963.

Weil, Louis. *Sacraments and Liturgy: The Outward Signs.* Oxford: Basil Blackwell, 1983.

Wheatly, Charles. *A Rational Illustration of the Book of Common Prayer of the Church of England.* Oxford: Oxford University Press, 1846; 1st ed., 1710.